LAUBACH WAY TO
ENGLISH

TEACHER'S MANUAL **3**

FOR SKILL BOOK

LAUBACH WAY TO READING

Jeanette D. Macero

Use with:

- Laubach Way to Reading: *Teacher's Manual for Skill Book 3*
  for reading and writing skills

New Readers Press
Publishing Division of
Laubach Literacy International

Materials needed for this level of the Laubach Way to English series:

For the teacher

- Laubach Way to English: *ESL Teacher's Manual for Skill Book 3* (for listening and speaking skills)

- Laubach Way to English: *ESL Illustrations for Skill Book 3* (to aid in teaching new vocabulary)

- Laubach Way to Reading: *Teacher's Manual for Skill Book 3* (for reading and writing skills)

- *The Laubach Way to Cursive Writing Teacher's Guide*

For the student

- Laubach Way to Reading: *Skill Book 3 Long Vowel Sounds* (text-workbook in reading and writing)

- *The Laubach Way to Cursive Writing* (student workbook, needed beginning in Lesson 22)

- Laubach Way to Reading: *Changes* (correlated reader to follow *Skill Book 3,* needed for Lessons 23 and 24)

- Laubach Way to Reading: *Checkups for Skill Book 3* (evaluation of student's progress in reading and writing, needed following Lesson 24)

EACH ONE TEACH ONE

ISBN 0-88336-395-X

© 1985, 1991

New Readers Press
Publishing Division of
Laubach Literacy International
Box 131, Syracuse, New York 13210

Printed in the United States of America

20   19   18   17   16   15   14   13   12   11
10   9   8   7   6   5   4   3

Table of Contents

Introduction

The Laubach Way to English is a series of teacher's manuals designed for teaching English to speakers of other languages (ESOL). Each teacher's manual is correlated to a skill book in the Laubach Way to Reading series. The skill book is the student's text-workbook in reading and writing. The materials provide a comprehensive beginning English program in listening, speaking, reading, and writing skills.

The Laubach Way to Reading series

The Laubach Way to Reading series is a basic reading and writing series, developed primarily for adults with little or no reading ability. The series, which begins at the zero level of literacy, consists of four skill books. Each skill book is followed by a correlated reader that gives additional practice in sustained reading.

```
* * * * * * * * * * * * * * * * * * * * * * * * * * * *
*                                                     *
*     The Laubach Way to Reading series               *
*                                                     *
*     Skill Book 1: Sounds and Names of Letters       *
*     Skill Book 2: Short Vowel Sounds                *
*     Skill Book 3: Long Vowel Sounds                 *
*     Skill Book 4: Other Vowel Sounds and            *
*                   Consonant Spellings               *
*                                                     *
* * * * * * * * * * * * * * * * * * * * * * * * * * * *
```

Components needed for level 3

The student's reading materials for this level are Skill Book 3 and the correlated reader Changes. Two teacher's manuals are required:

To teach listening and speaking skills at level 3, use the ESOL Conversation Skills Teacher's Manual for Skill Book 3 in the Laubach Way to English series. Practice in listening-and-speaking conversation skills includes dialogs, vocabulary, grammatical structures, and listening exercises. These skills are sequenced systematically so that the student has thorough aural-oral practice with vocabulary and grammatical structures before meeting them in the reading. Additional vocabulary and structures, not found in the reading, are provided for their usefulness in everyday life. ESOL Illustrations for Skill Book 3, a teacher's picture book, should be used in conjunction with this manual to show the student the meaning of new vocabulary.

To teach reading and writing skills, use the Teacher's Manual for Skill Book 3 in the Laubach Way to Reading series. It is written for all students using the skill books--both native speakers and ESOL students--so you may need to adapt the suggested teacher's instructions to the student somewhat for your ESOL student's comprehension.

Cursive writing is also taught at this level, beginning in Lesson 22. For this, you will need the student workbook The Laubach Way to Cursive Writing and the accompanying teacher's guide. For students who already know cursive writing, the LWR Teacher's Manual for Skill Book 3 provides alternative writing lessons.

Two evaluations of student progress complete level 3. The "Oral Evaluation of Skill Book 3," which checks the student's progress in conversation skills, is found at the end of this manual. To evaluate the student's progress in reading and writing, use the separate booklet Checkups for Skill Book 3. Directions for administering and scoring these checkups are at the end of the LWR Teacher's Manual for Skill Book 3.

A summary of the components needed for student and teacher at level 3 is provided on page 2 (the copyright page) of this manual.

Meeting the needs of ESOL students

The skill books were originally written for adult native speakers of English with little or no reading skill. The Laubach Way to English teacher's manuals were developed to adapt the skill books for ESOL instruction. The ESOL manuals for levels 1 and 2, besides providing instruction in conversation skills, also adapted the instructions for teaching reading and writing to the easy wording that beginning ESOL students could understand. (Level 3 students, in contrast, should be able to understand the verbal instructions suggested in the regular LWR Teacher's Manual for Skill Book 3 with only a little adaptation.)

When the reading series was revised for the edition called the Laubach Way to Reading, the author of this manual, Jeanette D. Macero, served as linguistic consultant to ensure that vocabulary and grammatical structures were introduced systematically in the skill books for the benefit of ESOL students.

Although the materials were designed specifically for teaching adults who are illiterate in their native language as well as in English, they can be used successfully with many other ESOL students. In particular, literate students whose native languages have writing systems other than the Roman alphabet should find the practice in basic reading and writing skills beneficial.

Each One Teach One, and classrooms too

Among other things, the "Laubach method" has traditionally meant "Each One Teach One," a volunteer tutor and a student, teaching and learning in an atmosphere of caring and compassion.

Accordingly, the methods described in the Laubach Way to English apply to a one-to-one teaching situation, but suggestions are offered for adapting the methods for small-group or classroom use. Thus, the series is useful for ESOL-ABE classes in public schools as well as for tutoring programs.

For volunteer tutors and beginning teachers

The detailed step-by-step instructions in both the Laubach Way to English and the Laubach Way to Reading teacher's manuals make it possible for both volunteer tutors and beginning ESOL teachers to use the material with ease and confidence.

Lesson 1

OBJECTIVES

When a student completes this unit, he should be able to:

1. Say and respond to a new dialog.
2. Say the chart words plus some words concerning music.
3. Recognize some music.
4. Say the names of animals and meats derived from the animals.
5. Say some story words, especially food items.
6. Use some irregular verbs in past tense statements.
7. Listen to a story and repeat it in his own words.

TEACHING AIDS

1. ESOL Illustrations for Skill Book 3, pp. 2-4.
2. A tape or record of a song.

I. Conversation Skills

DIALOG

David:	What are you going to order?
Jason:	I'm not very hungry. I'll have a snack.
David:	I won't eat much either. I'm on a diet.
Jason:	Sounds good. Here comes the waitress.
Waitress:	May I take your order?
David:	I'll have a salad and a diet soda.
Jason:	I'll have a ham sandwich and a cup of coffee.
Waitress:	Anything else?
Jason:	Not for now. Thanks.

Note: The procedure for teaching the dialog is the same as in the ESOL Manuals for Skill Books 1 and 2.

1. Model the entire dialog two or three times while the student listens.
   a. Do not say the words David, Jason, or Waitress.
   b. Explain vocabulary the student may not know; for example, on a diet means to eat less, to get thinner.
   c. Indicate appropriate pictures of a salad, a sandwich, and a soda as they occur in the dialog.
   d. To change roles, shift your weight from one foot to the other, and turn your body slightly.

2. Model each line of the dialog, having the student repeat it after you.
   Class: In a class situation, first have the class repeat in unison. Then divide the class into groups, and have each group repeat. Have members of the class begin each line of the dialog exactly at the same time, or there will be utter confusion.

3. Take one role of the dialog, and have the student take the others.

4. Reverse roles.

Class: For steps 3-4, have the members of the class say the dialog in unison, then in pairs. In a large class, divide the class in half, with each half taking first one, then the other role in the dialog. Then divide the class into quarters, ending with one-to-one practice. (In a dialog like this one with three speakers, divide the class into three groups, then six, and end with one-to-one practice.)

Keep the pace brisk. Praise your students often.

VOCABULARY: Music

I listen to music on the radio.
The singer is singing a song.
The song is _____.

---

1. Teacher models the sentences and plays a song. Student listens.

   Note: Teacher explains the vocabulary by indicating the singer and the name of the song being played.

2. Teacher models each sentence. Student repeats after each sentence.

   Note: You may sing the words of the song or play a tape or record of it. You may use songs such as "You are My Sunshine," "Clementine," or some current popular song. Avoid songs with difficult vocabulary, however.

3. Teacher and student sing the song together.

VOCABULARY: Meat and Animals

This is a lamb.
This is a cow.
This is a pig.
This is a chicken.
We eat the meat from these animals.

We eat beef. Beef and hamburger come from cows.
We eat pork and ham. Pork and ham come from pigs.
We eat lamb. It comes from lambs.
We eat chicken. It comes from chickens.

---

1. Teacher models all the sentences, using ESOL Illustrations 3, pp. 2-3.
2. Teacher models the sentences. Student repeats each sentence.

DRILL: Identification Drill

Teacher points to the illustrations and asks, "What's this?" Also, teacher asks, "Where do beef and hamburger come from?" and similar questions.

VOCABULARY: Food Items

Mrs. Falco goes to the supermarket to buy food for three meals:
   breakfast, lunch, and dinner.

She buys eggs, milk, and butter for breakfast.
She buys bread, ham, and cheese to make sandwiches for lunch.
She buys hamburger, beans, coffee, and tea for dinner.
She buys lettuce and tomatoes for a salad.

The food costs $30.00. The price of the food is $30.00.
Mrs. Falco pays her bill and goes home.

---

1. Teacher models each sentence, using actual objects
   or the pictures on pp. 4-5 of ESOL Illustrations 3.
   Student listens.

2. Teacher models each sentence, having the student repeat.

DRILL: Identification Drill

Teacher has student identify food items by asking the student "What's this?"
and using the objects or pictures on pp. 4-5 of ESOL Illustrations 3.

Note: Prompt the student only when necessary.
Review all previous words after each new word.

DRILL: Question and Answer Drill

Teacher asks questions to elicit vocabulary items. The student does not have
to name every item that would be a correct answer.

Model the first two items, having the student repeat only the answer.

Teacher	Student

Why does Mrs. Falco go to the supermarket?
She goes to buy food for breakfast,
   lunch, and dinner.
	She goes to buy food for breakfast,
	   lunch, and dinner.

What does Mrs. Falco buy for lunch? She buys bread, ham, and cheese.	She buys bread, ham, and cheese.

What kind of sandwiches will Mrs. Falco make?
What does Mrs. Falco buy for dinner?
What does Mrs. Falco buy to make a salad?
What does Mrs. Falco buy to drink?

Why does Mrs. Falco buy lettuce and tomatoes?
How much does the food cost?
How much was Mrs. Falco's bill?
What is the price of the food?

STRUCTURE FOCUS: Past Tense of Irregular Verbs

Present   Past

   Carla Lopez sends a letter   Carla Lopez sent a letter
      to her mother every week,   to her mother last week,
   I spend $1.00 to ride the bus   I spent $1.00 to ride the bus
      every week,   last week,
   Jason lends his book to David   Jason lent his book to David
      every week,   last week,

   Carla cuts the grass   Carla cut the grass
      every week,   two weeks ago,
   He puts money in the bank   He put $10.00 in the bank
      every week,   last week,
   He shuts the door   He shut the door
      when he comes in,   when he came in,

---

1. Teacher models each pair of sentences, saying first the present tense and
   then the past tense. Act out verbs the student does not know.
   Student listens,

2. Teacher models each sentence. Student repeats after each sentence,

Note: Be sure the student notices that there is only an _s ending difference
between the third person present and past tense forms of cost, cut, shut, and
put,

DRILL: Transformation Drill

Teacher gives a present tense statement.
Student changes it into a past tense statement,

Teacher   Student

I send a letter to my mother
   every week,
I sent a letter to my mother   I sent a letter to my mother
   last week,   last week,

Ed cuts the grass every week,
Ed cut the grass last week,   Ed cut the grass last week,

I lend my car to Jason.
The book costs $8.95 now.
Ed cuts the grass every week.
She puts her glasses in her purse.
Jason sends a letter to Ed every week.
Carla lends her jacket to Ann.
Ed shuts the door every day.

DRILL: Answering Questions

Teacher asks student questions which he answers in the past tense.

Teacher   Student

What did David lend Tom?
He lent him a book.   He lent him a book.

What did you send your mother?
I sent her some money.   I sent her some money.

Where did you put your coat?
What did you lend Carla?
How much did the book cost?
Who cut the bread?
How much did Jason spend for food?
When did you lend Carla your book?
When did Ed shut the door?

<u>STRUCTURE FOCUS</u>: <u>before</u> and <u>after</u>

<u>Before</u> work, I had breakfast.
<u>Before</u> watching TV, I had dinner.
<u>Before</u> class, I read my book.

<u>After</u> work, I had dinner.
<u>After</u> watching TV, I went to bed.
<u>After</u> class, I went home.

---

1. Teacher models each sentence, asking the student to listen to <u>before</u> or <u>after</u>. Student listens.

2. Teacher models each sentence. Student repeats after each sentence.

<u>DRILL</u>: <u>Question and Answer Drill</u>

Teacher asks these questions: "What did you do <u>before</u> class?" and "What did you do <u>after</u> class?" Student replies <u>may</u> vary.

<u>Teacher</u>	<u>Student</u>
What did you do before class? I read my book before class.	I read my book before class.
What did you do after eating a snack? I went to bed after eating a snack.	I went to bed after eating a snack.

What did you do before work?
What did you do before class?
What did you do before dinner?
What did you do before watching TV?
What did you do before going to bed?

What did you do after work?
What did you do after class?
What did you do after dinner?
What did you do after watching TV?
What did you do after eating a snack?

<u>LISTENING COMPREHENSION</u>

Jason and Carla went to Fran's Snack Shop. They were hungry. Jason ordered a ham sandwich. They both drank milk. They said the food was good.

---

1. Teacher reads the story twice at a normal pace. Student listens. Student asks about words he does not know.

2. Student tells the story in his own words. If the student cannot tell the story, teacher may begin the sentence and have the student complete it.

ORAL EVALUATION

It is recommended that the teacher have a notebook for recording the student's progress. It is especially necessary to make notes about items that a student is having difficulty with so that you can review the items at the beginning of the next session.

When possible, the number of vocabulary items the student should be able to name is indicated. For most reviews of structure focus drills, the student should be able to respond fairly quickly. If he needs prompting to any great extent, make a note, and review the structure at the next session.

Follow these procedures for the oral evaluation at the end of each lesson.

1. Have the student say the words about music and say the words of the song (if you taught a song).

2. Using ESOL Illustrations 3, pp. 2-3, have the student identify the names of the animals and the meats derived from them by doing the Identification Drill. Student should be able to name 8 items.

3. Using ESOL Illustrations 3, pp. 4-5, do the Question and Answer Drill about food items. Student should be able to name 7 items.

4. Have the student review the present and past tense of irregular verbs by doing the Transformation Drill. Student should know the past tense of each verb.

II. Reading and Writing

SKILL BOOK 3: Lesson 1

Complete Lesson 1 in Skill Book 3, following the instructions given in the Laubach Way to Reading Teacher's Manual for Skill Book 3. Adapt the wording of the suggested teacher's instructions to the student as needed for your ESOL student's comprehension.

ADDITIONAL WRITTEN PRACTICE

After completing Lesson 1 in the skill book, have the student do the practices for Lesson 1 in the Workbook for Skill Book 3.

Note: The Workbook for Skill Book 3 is designed to give ESOL students in particular additional practice in the patterns presented in Skill Book 3. The vocabulary is controlled to the reading vocabulary the student has learned at each lesson level in Skill Book 3, although some new words are introduced. Before assigning any material in the Workbook for Skill Book 3, read the introductory section called "To the Teacher" for an explanation of how to use the exercises.

Lesson 2

OBJECTIVES

When a student completes this unit, he should be able to:

1. Say and respond to a new dialog.
2. Say some words about work.
3. Say some names of vegetables.
4. Say some liquid measures and food in quantities.
5. Use the structure it + be, as in It's sunny.
6. Use the structure it for identification, as in Who is it? It's Ed.
7. Use the present perfect tense with ever and never.
8. Listen to a story and repeat it in his own words.

VISUAL AIDS

1. ESOL Illustrations 3, pp. 4-8.

2. Bring some rice, plus color pictures of these vegetables or the actual vegetables:

   tomatoes   carrots   onions   beans
   lettuce   potatoes   peas

3. Measuring cup that shows 1/4 and 1/2 cup markings.

I. Conversation Skills

DIALOG

Carla:	I don't know what to cook for dinner tonight.
Mrs. King:	How about chicken with instant rice and a salad?
Carla:	What's instant rice?
Mrs. King:	It's rice that cooks very fast. It's easy to cook.
Carla:	It sounds good.
	Would you like to have dinner with us?
Mrs. King:	No, thanks. Not tonight. I have to work.

1. Model the entire dialog two or three times. Student listens.
2. Model each line. Student repeats after each line.
3. Teacher takes one role of the dialog. Student takes the other.
4. Reverse roles.
5. Vary the dialog by practicing with other menus the student may suggest.

VOCABULARY: Words about Work

Ray has a <u>full-time</u> job in a paper factory.
He works 40 hours a week.

Kay has two <u>part-time</u> jobs.

She is a <u>baby-sitter</u>.
She baby-sits for 15 hours every week.

She is a <u>clerk</u> in a department store.
She works there 15 hours every week.

---

1. While student listens, teacher models each sentence, using <u>ESOL</u> <u>Illustrations 3</u>, p. 8, to show the new words <u>baby-sitter</u> and <u>clerk</u>. Explain that a full-time job is 35-40 hours of work per week, and a part-time job is less than that.

2. Teacher models the sentences. Student repeats after each sentence.

VOCABULARY: Vegetables

Many people eat <u>vegetables</u>.
They eat <u>tomatoes</u>.
They eat <u>lettuce</u>.
They eat <u>carrots</u>.
They eat <u>potatoes</u>.
They eat <u>peas</u>.
They eat <u>onions</u>.
They eat <u>rice</u>.
They eat <u>beans</u>.

<u>Note</u>: You may wish to add other vegetables, depending on what foods are part of your student's diet, e.g., eggplant, corn, cabbage, cucumber, celery, or green pepper.

1. Teacher models each sentence, using rice and other actual vegetables, color photos, or <u>ESOL Illustrations 3</u>, pp. 4-7, to show the new words.

2. Teacher models the sentences. Student repeats after each sentence.

DRILL: Identification Drill

Teacher points to the illustrations of vegetables and asks, "What's this?" or "What do people eat?"

VOCABULARY: Liquid Measures

This is a cup.
This is a half cup.
This is a quarter cup.
---

1. Teacher models each sentence, using a measuring cup or ESOL Illustrations 3, p. 7, to show the new words.

2. Teacher models the sentences. Student repeats after each sentence.

VOCABULARY: Food in Quantities

Mrs. Falco buys a stick of butter.
She puts a pat of butter on her bread.
She buys a head of lettuce.
She buys a can of peas.
She buys a pound of hamburger.
She buys a quart of milk.
---

1. While student listens, teacher models each sentence, using actual objects or ESOL Illustrations 3, pp. 4-7, to show the new words.

2. Teacher models the sentences. Student repeats after each sentence.

<u>STRUCTURE FOCUS</u>: <u>It</u> + <u>be</u>

> <u>It's</u> half past six.
> <u>It's</u> a nice day today. It's sunny.
> <u>It was</u> rainy yesterday.
> <u>It's</u> June.
> <u>It's</u> fun to play cards.

---

1. Teacher models each sentence, asking the student to listen to <u>It's</u> and <u>It was</u>.

2. Teacher models the sentence. Student repeats after each sentence.

<u>DRILL</u>: <u>Completion Drill</u>

1. Teacher gives part of a sentence.
   Student completes the sentences by using <u>It's</u> and <u>It was</u>.

2. Teacher models the first two items. Student listens.

<u>Note</u>: Conduct each drill in this book in this manner. These instructions will not be repeated for each drill after this.

<u>Teacher</u>	<u>Student</u>
half past six	
It's half past six.	It's half past six.
sunny yesterday	
It was sunny yesterday.	It was sunny yesterday.

rainy today
June
Monday
7 o'clock
easy to play cards
hard to make ice cream
fun to go fishing yesterday
easy to make a cake
a nice day today

STRUCTURE FOCUS: <u>It</u> for Identification

Who is <u>it</u> at the door?   <u>It's</u> Carla and David.
Who was <u>it</u> on the telephone?   <u>It</u> was Anne.

---

1. Teacher models each question with its answer. Student listens.
2. Teacher models each question and answer. Student repeats after each item.

DRILL: Completion Drill

Teacher gives part of a sentence.
Student completes the sentence by using <u>It's</u> or <u>It was</u>.

Teacher	Student
Ed It's Ed.	It's Ed.
Carla and David It's Carla and David.	It's Carla and David.

Anne on the telephone yesterday
a woman at the door
a man on the telephone last night
your mother
your sister and brother
me
Rosa on the telephone
Jason at the door last night

STRUCTURE FOCUS: Present Perfect Tense with ever and never

Have you ever painted a house?
No, I have never painted a house.

Have you ever fixed stairs?
No, I have never fixed stairs.

Have you ever spent $200 for food?
No, I have never spent $200 for food.

Have you ever sent a letter to the president?
No, I have never sent a letter to the president.

Have you ever lent anyone your car?
No, I have never lent anyone my car.

---

1. Teacher models the sentences in pairs, the question with ever and the answer with never.

2. Teacher models each question and its answer. Student repeats after each item.

DRILL: Answering Questions

Teacher asks student questions with ever which he answers in the negative with never.

Teacher	Student
Have you ever painted your house?	
No, I have never painted my house.	No, I have never painted my house.
Have you ever fixed stairs?	
No, I have never fixed stairs.	No, I have never fixed stairs.
Have you ever sent Carla a letter?	
Have you ever lent Ed any money?	
Have you ever spent a lot of money in one day?	
Have you ever lent anyone your car?	
Have you ever lived in New York?	
Have you ever lived in a big apartment?	
Have you ever washed a dog?	
Have you ever painted stairs?	

DRILL: Making Questions

Teacher gives words which student must use in the question form
Have you ever...?

Teacher   Student

painted a house
Have you ever painted a house?   Have you ever painted a house?

fixed stairs
Have you ever fixed stairs?   Have you ever fixed stairs?

spent a lot of money
sent Carla a letter
lent Ed some money
fixed a chair
lived in New York
washed a dog

Note: Drill can be varied by having student make questions about Jason:
"Has Jason ever painted a house?" Continue with the remaining items.

LISTENING COMPREHENSION

          Carla Lopez lives in an apartment in a big building.
      She works at a music shop. She has worked there for six
      years.
          Carla has a baby. Her baby's name is Rosa. Rosa is two.
      Mrs. King is Rosa's baby-sitter. She baby-sits with Rosa
      while Carla is at work.
----

1. Teacher reads the story twice at a normal pace.
   Student listens. Student asks about words he does not know.

2. Student tells the story in his own words. If the student cannot tell
   the story, teacher may begin the sentence and have the student complete it.

Note: If the student cannot remember the story, read it once or twice again.

ORAL EVALUATION

1. Using ESOL Illustrations 3, p. 8, have your student identify the words about work. He should be able to identify all of them.

2. Using ESOL Illustrations 3, pp. 4-6, have your student identify the vegetables. He should be able to name 7 of them fairly quickly.

3. Using ESOL Illustrations 3, p. 7, have your student identify the liquid measures. He should be able to name all of them.

4. Using ESOL Illustrations 3, pp. 4-7, have your student identify foods in quantity. He should be able to name 5 of them.

5. Review the present perfect tense with ever and never. Do the drill on making questions, and have the student answer.

II. Reading and Writing

SKILL BOOK 3: Lesson 2

Complete Lesson 2 in Skill Book 3, following the instructions given in the Laubach Way to Reading Teacher's Manual for Skill Book 3. Adapt the wording of the suggested teacher's instructions to the student as needed for your ESOL student's comprehension.

Note: In this lesson and following lessons, you may need especially to adapt the oral comprehension questions suggested for each story. You may need to change the wording or to explain the meaning of any new vocabulary items or of idioms that your ESOL student does not understand.

At times, you may need to explain some facet of American culture. For example, one question about the story in Lesson 2 asks, "Do you think the baby-sitter is about the same age as Carla or much older?" The answer is that the baby-sitter is probably much older because Carla calls her Mrs. instead of using her first name. Your ESOL student may need to be told that American acquaintances of about the same age usually call each other by their first names, even if they are not very close friends. We usually use titles like Mr. and Mrs. only for persons who are much older or are in a much higher position.

If any oral comprehension question requires more explanation than you think its content is worth, feel free to omit it.

ADDITIONAL WRITTEN PRACTICE

After completing Lesson 2 in the skill book, have the student do the practices for Lesson 2 in the Workbook for Skill Book 3.

Lesson 3

OBJECTIVES

When a student completes this unit, he should be able to:

1. Say and respond to a new dialog.
2. Say words about getting paid and writing checks.
3. Use the verbs play + noun and go + verb-ing to indicate games and sports.
4. Use the structure have to.
5. Use It + adjective + infinitive, as in It is fun to go camping.
6. Listen to a story and repeat it in his own words.

VISUAL AIDS

1. ESOL Illustrations 3, pp. 9-13.
2. An example of a personal check. (An old cancelled check will do.)

I. Conversation Skills

DIALOG

A: Hello, I'm calling about the apartment you advertised in the paper. How many bedrooms are there?
B: Two. There's a big living room and a modern kitchen.

A: How much is it a month?
B: It's $300 a month plus utilities.

A: I'd like to think it over. I'll call you back.

---

1. Model the entire dialog two or three times. Student listens.

   Note: Explain that utilities include stove, lights, heat.
   The word plus means "and" or "in addition to."

2. Model each line. Student repeats after each line.
3. Teacher takes one role of the dialog. Student takes the other.
4. Reverse roles.

VOCABULARY: Getting Paid and Writing Checks

Kay and Ray Mason have jobs.
They get paid <u>twice</u> a month.
They get $500 every <u>payday</u>.

Kay writes a <u>check</u> for their telephone bill.
Kay writes a <u>check</u> for the <u>rent</u>.
Kay gives the rent check to the <u>landlady</u>.

---

1. Teacher models each sentence, using <u>ESOL</u> <u>Illustrations</u> <u>3</u>, p. 9.
   Student listens.

2. Teacher models the sentences. Student repeats after each sentence.

DRILL: Question and Answer Drill

Teacher asks questions to elicit vocabulary items.

Teacher	Student
Who has a job?	
Kay and Ray Mason.	Kay and Ray Mason.
How often do Kay and Ray get paid?	
They get paid twice a month.	They get paid twice a month.

How much do Kay and Ray get every payday?
How do they pay their telephone bill?
Who do they pay their rent to?
When do Kay and Ray get five hundred dollars?
How often do Kay and Ray get paid?

<u>VOCABULARY</u>: <u>The Verbs</u> <u>play</u> <u>and</u> <u>go</u> <u>with Games and Sports</u>

<u>play</u>	<u>go</u>
They play cards.	They go camping.
They play football.	They go fishing.
They play baseball.	They go swimming.
They play basketball.	They go skiing.
They play hockey.	They go skating.

1. Teacher models all the sentences with <u>play</u>, then those with <u>go</u>. Use <u>ESOL</u> <u>Illustrations</u> <u>3</u>, pp. 10-13. Student listens.

2. Teacher models each sentence. Student repeats after each sentence.

<u>Note</u>: Some activities are expressed with <u>play</u> + noun, others with <u>go</u> + verb-<u>ing</u>. Student may ask you about other sports he knows.

<u>DRILL</u>: <u>Completing Sentences</u>

Teacher names an activity. Student uses it in a sentence with <u>play</u> or <u>go</u>.

<u>Teacher</u>	<u>Student</u>
cards	
We play cards.	We play cards.
camping	
We go camping.	We go camping.

football
basketball
swimming
fishing
skiing
baseball
skating
hockey

STRUCTURE FOCUS: <u>have to</u> + <u>Simple Form of the Verb</u>

I	<u>have</u> <u>to</u>	<u>eat</u>	dinner after work.
You	<u>have</u> <u>to</u>	<u>stop</u>	for a red light.
He	<u>has</u> <u>to</u>	<u>call</u>	Carla before dinner.
We	<u>have</u> <u>to</u>	<u>work</u>	tomorrow.

1. Teacher models each sentence, asking the student to listen to <u>have to</u> and <u>has to</u>.

2. Teacher models each sentence. Student repeats after each sentence.

DRILL: Question and Answer Drill

Teacher asks a question which the student answers using <u>have to</u>. Student replies may vary.

Teacher	Student
What do you have to do after breakfast?	
I have to go to work.	I have to go to work.
What do you have to do tomorrow?	
I have to buy some food.	I have to buy some food.

What do you have to do after dinner?
What do you have to do after work?
What do you have to do today?
What do you have to do tomorrow?
What do you have to do after class?
What do you have to do before dinner?

STRUCTURE FOCUS: <u>It</u> + <u>Adjective</u> + <u>Infinitive</u>

It	is	fun	to go	camping.
It	is	easy	to play	cards.
It	is	hard	to pay	our bills.
It	is	nice	to be	with friends.

1. Teacher models each sentence, asking student to listen to <u>to go</u>, <u>to play</u>, etc. Student listens.

2. Teacher models each sentence. Student repeats after each sentence.

DRILL: Making Questions

Teacher gives words which student must use in the question form <u>Is it...?</u> Student completes the question.

Teacher	Student
fun to go camping	
Is it fun to go camping?	Is it fun to go camping?
easy to play cards	
Is it easy to play cards?	Is it easy to play cards?
fun to go fishing	
hard to pay your bills	
nice to be with friends	
fun to go camping	
easy to play baseball	

LISTENING COMPREHENSION

Kay and Ray Mason like to play cards with their friends. They sometimes play cards with Carla and David. They have fun together.

Sometimes Kay and Ray go camping. They go camping in the woods. They go fishing. They have fun together.

---

1. Teacher reads the story twice at a normal pace. Student listens. Student asks about words he does not know.

2. Student tells the story in his own words. If the student cannot tell the story, teacher may begin the sentence and have the student complete it.

Note: If the student cannot remember the story, read it once or twice again.

ORAL EVALUATION

1. Using ESOL Illustrations 3, p. 9, have the student identify the words about getting paid and writing checks by doing the Question and Answer Drill. Student should be able to answer all the questions.

2. Using ESOL Illustrations 3, pp. 10-13, name the activity and have the student use it in a sentence with play or go. Student should know 6 of them.

3. Review have to + simple form of the verb by doing the Question and Answer Drill.

4. Review It + adjective + infinitive by doing the Making Questions Drill.

II. Reading and Writing

SKILL BOOK 3: Lesson 3

Complete Lesson 3 in Skill Book 3, following the instructions given in the Laubach Way to Reading Teacher's Manual for Skill Book 3. Adapt the wording of the suggested teacher's instructions to the student as needed for your ESOL student's comprehension.

ADDITIONAL WRITTEN PRACTICE

After completing Lesson 3 in the skill book, have the student do the practices for Lesson 3 in the Workbook for Skill Book 3.

Lesson 4

<u>OBJECTIVES</u>

When a student completes this unit, he should be able to:

1. Say and respond to a new dialog.
2. Say some words about basic tools and equipment.
3. Say the parts of the face.
4. Use <u>shall</u> in questions.
5. Use <u>when</u> clauses.
6. Use <u>verb</u> + infinitive, as in <u>I'll plan to go.</u>
7. Use verb + noun/pronoun + infinitive, as in <u>I'll ask them to come.</u>
8. Listen to a story and repeat it in his own words.

<u>VISUAL AIDS</u>

1. <u>ESOL Illustrations 3</u>, pp. 14-16.
2. Any of these objects that it is convenient to bring:

hammer	pliers	saw	pail
nails	ladder	piece of wood	paint
screwdriver		scissors	paintbrush
screws		paper	

<u>I. Conversation Skills</u>

<u>DIALOG</u>

A: I want to fix this chair. It's broken.
B: You'll need a hammer and some nails.

A: I'll buy the nails at the store.
   Will you help me fix the chair?
B: Sure. I'll be glad to.

Use actual objects or <u>ESOL Illustrations 3</u>, pp. 14-15.

1. Model the entire dialog two or three times. Student listens.
2. Model each line. Student repeats after each line.
3. Teacher takes one role of the dialog. Student takes the other.
4. Reverse roles.

<u>Note</u>: Follow the same procedure for all dialogs in the following lessons.

VOCABULARY: Basic Tools and Equipment

> We need a hammer and some nails.
> We need a screwdriver and some screws.
> We need a saw to cut wood.
> We need pliers.
> We need scissors to cut paper.
> We need a ladder to climb to high places.
> We need a pail to put water in.
> We need some paint and a brush.

Use actual objects or ESOL Illustrations 3, pp. 14-15.

1. Teacher models each sentence. Student listens.
2. Teacher models the sentences. Student repeats after each sentence.

Note: Follow the same procedure for all Vocabulary and Structure Focus sections of the lessons from now on.

DRILL: Identification Drill

Teacher holds up an object or points to picture on ESOL Illustrations 3, p. 16, and asks, "What's this?"

Note: Prompt only when necessary. Review all previous words after each new word.

VOCABULARY: Parts of the Face

> Carla has a pretty face.
> She has black hair.
> She has brown eyes.
> She has red lips.
> She has pink cheeks.
> She has nice teeth.
> She has small ears.

Use ESOL Illustrations 3, p. 16.

DRILL: Identification Drill

Point to different parts of the illustration of the face and ask, "What's this?" Prompt only when necessary.

STRUCTURE FOCUS: The Use of shall

Shall I pick you up after work?   Yes, thank you.
Shall we take the children with us?   No, let's not.
Shall we fix the stairs first?   Yes, let's.
Shall we go away at the end of the month?   Yes, I'd like to.
Shall we have a cup of coffee?   No, not now.
Shall I invite David to come to dinner?   Yes, please do.

Note: The word Shall is used with I and we in polite questions and in questions asking for advice.

DRILL: Making Questions

Teacher gives part of a question.
Student completes the question using Shall I or Shall we.

Teacher   Student

pick you up after work
Shall I pick you up after work?   Shall I pick you up after work?

ask David to come to dinner
Shall we ask David to come to dinner?   Shall we ask David to come to dinner?

fix the table
go away at the end of the month
have a cup of coffee
play baseball
watch TV
play cards

DRILL: Answering Questions

Teacher asks a question with Shall I or Shall we.
Student gives an appropriate affirmative or negative reply.
Encourage the student to use the various replies introduced.

Teacher   Student

Shall I pick you up after work?
Yes, thank you.   Yes, thank you.

Shall we have a cup of coffee?
No, not now.   No, not now.

Shall we fix the stairs first?
Shall we play cards?
Shall I pick you up after work?
Shall I ask Mrs. King to baby-sit?
Shall I ask Carla to come to dinner?
Shall we paint the kitchen?

STRUCTURE FOCUS: When Clauses

When Carla calls, I will talk to her.
When the telephone rings, I will answer it.
When the teacher talks, I will listen to her.

Model each sentence, asking the student to listen to when.

Note: The when clause uses the simple present tense,
and the main clause uses will.

DRILL: Completion Drill

Teacher gives the when clause.
Student completes the sentence using a main clause with will.

Teacher	Student
When Carla calls	
When Carla calls,	When Carla calls,
I will talk to her.	I will talk to her.
When the telephone rings	
When the telephone rings,	When the telephone rings,
I will answer it.	I will answer it.

When the teacher talks
When David goes to class
When Kay pays her bills
When Gail fixes the chair
When Jason paints the chair
When class starts

STRUCTURE FOCUS: Verb + Infinitive

	Verb	Infinitive
I'll	learn	to speak English in this class.
I'll	wait	to go home with Kay.
I'll	remember	to get some milk after class.
I'll	ask	to go.

As you model each sentence, have the student listen to to speak, to go, and so on.

Note: The verbs used have been introduced previously except for wait and remember.

DRILL: Completion Drill

Teacher gives the beginning of the sentence, which the student must complete using an infinitive. Student replies may vary.

Teacher	Student
I'll ask	
I'll ask to go.	I'll ask to go.
I'll learn	
I'll learn to read in this class.	I'll learn to read in this class.

Teacher

I'll need	I'll remember	I'll ask
I'll plan	I'll wait	I'll learn

STRUCTURE FOCUS: Verb + Object (Noun/Pronoun) + Infinitive

	Verb	Object	Infinitive
I'll	ask	Carla	to help me.
I'll	invite	Kay and Ray	to come with me.
I'll	order	them	to go.
I'll	teach	them	to read.
I'll	tell	them	to stop.
I'll	want	him	to help us.

As you model the sentences, explain that order means to force someone to do something.

DRILL: Completion Drill

Teacher gives the beginning of the sentence, which the student must complete using a noun or pronoun and an infinitive. Student replies may vary.

Teacher   Student

I'll ask
I'll ask Carla to call you.   I'll ask Carla to call you.

I'll teach
I'll teach them to read.   I'll teach them to read.

Teacher

I'll ask   I'll order   I'll tell   I'll invite
I'll need   I'll teach   I'll want

DRILL: Completion Drill

Teacher gives the beginning of the sentence, which student must complete by using to do it or you to do it. (With want, ask, and need, both answers are correct.)

Teacher   Student

I'll learn
I'll learn to do it.   I'll learn to do it.

I'll order
I'll order you to do it. I'll order you to do it.

Teacher

I'll teach	I'll plan	I'll want	I'll need	I'll remember
I'll tell	I'll order	I'll ask	I'll learn	I'll wait
				I'll invite

LISTENING COMPREHENSION

Gail Fisher and Jason Hunt need to buy a hammer and some nails. They are going to fix the kitchen table. After they fix the table, they are going to paint it. They are going to paint the table black.

---

1. Teacher reads the story twice at a normal pace.
   Student listens. Student asks about words he does not know.

2. Student tells the story in his own words. If the student cannot tell the story, teacher may begin the sentence and have the student complete it.

Note: If the student cannot remember the story, read it once or twice again.

ORAL EVALUATION

1. Using ESOL Illustrations 3, pp. 14-15, have your student identify basic tools and equipment. He should be able to name 11 items.

2. Using ESOL Illustrations 3, p. 16, have your student identify parts of the face. He should know all of them.

3. Review shall by doing the drills on Making Questions and Answering Questions.

4. Review when clauses by doing the Completion Drill.

5. Review the verb + infinitive and verb + object + infinitive by doing the three Completion Drills.

II. Reading and Writing

SKILL BOOK 3: Lesson 4

Complete Lesson 4 in Skill Book 3, following the instructions given in the Laubach Way to Reading Teacher's Manual for Skill Book 3. Adapt the wording of the suggested teacher's instructions to the student as needed for your ESOL student's comprehension.

ADDITIONAL WRITTEN PRACTICE

After completing Lesson 4 in the skill book, have the student do the practices for Lesson 4 in the Workbook for Skill Book 3.

Lesson 5

OBJECTIVES

When a student completes this unit, he should be able to:

1. Say and respond to a new dialog.
2. Say some words about a wedding.
3. Say some words about taking pictures.
4. Say the past participle of the irregular verbs sing, ring, drink, give, forgive, eat.
5. Use already with the present perfect tense.
6. Use already and yet.
7. Use may for permission.
8. Use reflexive pronouns as objects, as in I hurt myself.
9. Use still and any more.
10. Use verb + gerund, as in He has quit working.
11. Listen to a story and repeat it in his own words.

VISUAL AIDS

1. ESOL Illustrations 3, pp. 17-19.
2. A small pocket mirror.

I. Conversation Skills

DIALOG

A: I'm invited to a lot of parties this month.
B: You are? How many?

A: Three. I'm invited to Jason's birthday party.
    I'm invited to a party for Gail before her wedding.
    And I'm invited to Jason and Gail's wedding.
B: You'll have to buy three gifts. What are you going to get?

A: I'll get Jason a book. I'll get Gail a pretty nightgown.
    I think I'll buy a silver tray for a wedding gift.
B: Sounds very nice. I'm sure they'll like everything.

A: I hope so.

Use the actual objects or ESOL Illustrations 3, p. 17, for pretty nightgown and silver tray.

VOCABULARY: A Wedding

Gail and Jason got married in church.
Many of their friends came to the wedding.
Jason's mother baked a cake for the wedding.
She put the cake on a pretty plate.

Use ESOL Illustrations 3, p. 18.

DRILL: Identification Drill

Teacher has student identify items by asking "What's this?"
and using the pictures on p. 18 of ESOL Illustrations 3.

VOCABULARY: Taking Pictures

Gail's uncle has an expensive camera that cost a lot of money.
He buys a lot of film to take pictures with.
When he takes a very good picture, he puts it in a frame.

Use ESOL Illustrations 3, p. 19.

DRILL: Identification Drill

Teacher has student identify items by asking "What's this?"
and using the pictures on p. 19 of ESOL Illustrations 3.

VOCABULARY: Past Participles of Irregular Verbs

I sing a song.
I sang a song.
I have sung many songs.

- - - - - - - - - - - - - -

sing	sang	have sung
ring	rang	have rung
drink	drank	have drunk
give	gave	have given
forgive	forgave	have forgiven
eat	ate	have eaten

---

1. Teacher models the first three sentences. Student listens and then repeats.
2. Teacher models all three forms of all the verbs. Student listens.
3. Teacher models all three forms of each verb.
   Student repeats after each set of three verb forms.

STRUCTURE FOCUS: <u>Present Perfect Tense with</u> <u>already</u>

Is she going to sing the song?
She has <u>already</u> sung the song.

Is the bell going to ring?
The bell has <u>already</u> rung.

Are you going to drink some coffee?
I've <u>already</u> drunk some coffee.

Are you going to give her the money?
I've <u>already</u> given her the money.

Are you going to forgive him for what he did?
I've <u>already</u> forgiven him for what he did.

Are you going to eat some cake?
I've <u>already</u> eaten some cake.

---

1. Teacher models each question and its answer, asking the student to listen to <u>already</u>. Student listens.

2. Teacher models each question and its answer.
   Student repeats only the answer with <u>already</u>.

STRUCTURE FOCUS: <u>The Use of</u> <u>already</u> <u>and</u> <u>yet</u>

She has <u>already</u> sung the song.
She hasn't sung the song <u>yet</u>.

The bell has <u>already</u> rung.
The bell hasn't rung <u>yet</u>.

I have <u>already</u> drunk some coffee.
I haven't drunk any coffee <u>yet</u>.

---

1. Teacher models the sentences in pairs with <u>already</u> and <u>yet</u>, asking the student to listen to <u>already</u> and <u>yet</u>. Student listens.

2. Teacher models the sentences in pairs with <u>already</u> and <u>yet</u>.
   Student repeats after each sentence.

Note: <u>Already</u> is often used in affirmative statements. <u>Yet</u> is used in negative statements.

DRILL: Expansion Drill

Teacher gives a statement to which the student adds already or yet.

Teacher   Student

She has sung the song.
She has already sung the song.   She has already sung the song.

The bell hasn't rung.
The bell hasn't rung yet.   The bell hasn't rung yet.

I have drunk some coffee.
I have given her the money.
I haven't forgiven him for what he did.
I have eaten a sandwich.
Jane hasn't sung a song.
The bell hasn't rung.
Carla hasn't drunk any diet soda.
David hasn't given me the book.

DRILL: Answering Questions

Teacher asks student a question which he answers
using already and the present perfect tense.

Teacher   Student

Is she going to sing the song?
She has already sung the song.   She has already sung the song.

Is the bell going to ring?
The bell has already rung.   The bell has already rung.

Are you going to drink a diet soda?
Are you going to give her a gift?
Are you going to forgive him for what he said?
Are you going to eat a sandwich?
Is Jane going to sing a song?
Is the bell going to ring?

STRUCTURE FOCUS: The Use of may for Permission

May I have some cake?	Yes, you may.
May I have a sandwich?	Yes, sure.
May I speak to Jane?	Yes, certainly.

Note: May is used to ask permission.
The reply Yes, you may is more formal than Sure or Certainly.

DRILL: Making Questions

Teacher gives part of a question. Student completes the question using May I.

Teacher	Student
have some cake	
May I have some cake?	May I have some cake?
speak to David	
May I speak to David?	May I speak to David?

have a sandwich
use your pen
have some cake
speak to Jane
take your picture
have a drink

DRILL: Answering Questions

Teacher asks a question with May I, which student answers with
Yes, you may or Sure or Certainly.

Teacher	Student
May I have some cake?	
Yes, you may.	Yes, you may.
May I speak to Jane?	
Yes, sure.	Yes, sure.
May I use your pen?	
Yes, certainly.	Yes, certainly.

May I have a sandwich?
May I speak to David?
May I take your picture?
May I have a drink?
May I use your pen?
May I see your book for a minute?

STRUCTURE FOCUS: Reflexive Pronouns as Objects

I look at myself in the mirror.
You look at yourself in the mirror.
He looks at himself in the mirror.
She looks at herself in the mirror.
The cat hurt itself.

We look at ourselves in the mirror.
You look at yourselves in the mirror.
They look at themselves in the mirror.

As you model the sentences, ask the student to listen to myself, yourself, and so on. Show the student a mirror.

DRILL: Substitution Drill

Teacher gives the subject pronoun.
Student gives the reflexive pronoun that is used with it.

Teacher   Student

I
myself   myself

you (three people)
yourselves   yourselves

Teacher

we   she   you (one)   they
he   it   we   you (two people)

DRILL: Answering Questions

Teacher asks questions which student answers using a reflexive pronoun.

Teacher   Student

Who are you talking to?
I'm talking to myself.   I'm talking to myself.

Who hurt the cat?
The cat hurt itself.   The cat hurt itself.

Who is Jane talking to?
Who are you reading to?
Who is Carla baking the cake for?
Who are you giving the book to?
Who is David buying the shirt for?
Who are they getting the books for?
Who hurt the cat?

STRUCTURE FOCUS: The Use of still and any more

They are still in church.
They aren't in church any more.

Carla is still at home.
Carla isn't at home any more.

As you model the sentences, ask the student to listen to still and any more.

Note: Still is used in affirmative statements.
Yet is used in negative statements.

DRILL: Expansion Drill

Teacher gives a sentence to which the student adds still or any more.

Teacher	Student

He is at home.
He is still at home.   He is still at home.

He isn't at home.
He isn't at home any more.   He isn't at home any more.

We see Gail at work.
We don't see Gail at work.

They live in New York.
They don't live in New York.

I have my car.
I don't have my car.

She works at the paper factory.
She doesn't work at the paper factory.

STRUCTURE FOCUS: Verb + Gerund

	Verb	Gerund
I've	finished	reading the book.
I've	stopped	talking to her.
He has	quit	working.

As you model the sentences, ask the student to listen to reading, talking, and working.

Note: The verbs quit and finish are new here.

DRILL: Completion Drill

Teacher gives the beginning of a sentence which student must complete using a gerund. Student replies may vary.

Teacher	Student
I've finished	
I've finished reading the book.	I've finished reading the book.
He has quit	
He has quit working.	He has quit working.
I've stopped	
He has quit	
He has practiced	
They have stopped	
We have finished	

LISTENING COMPREHENSION

Ed and Jane went to a wedding. First, they went to the church to see the wedding. After the wedding, they went to the wedding party.

At the party, there was a big wedding cake, sandwiches, coffee, and other drinks. Ed helped himself to a sandwich and coffee. Jane helped herself to a piece of the wedding cake.

---

1. Teacher reads the story twice at a normal pace.
   Student listens. Student asks about words he does not know.

2. Student tells the story in his own words. If the student cannot tell the story, teacher may begin the sentence and have the student complete it.

Note: If the student cannot remember the story, read it once or twice again.

ORAL EVALUATION

1. Using ESOL Illustrations 3, p. 18, have the student identify the words about a wedding. Student should know all of them.

2. Using ESOL Illustrations 3, p. 19, have the student identify the words about taking pictures. Student should know all of them.

3. Have the student say the past and past participle of the irregular verbs and use them with already in the present perfect tense. Student should know all of them.

4. Review already and yet by doing the Expansion Drill.

5. Review the use of may for permission by doing the drills on Making Questions and Answering Questions.

6. Review the use of the reflexive pronouns as objects by doing the drill on Answering Questions.

7. Review the use of still and any more by doing the Expansion Drill.

8. Review the use of verb + gerund by doing the Completion Drill.

II. Reading and Writing

SKILL BOOK 3: Lesson 5

Complete Lesson 5 in Skill Book 3, following the instructions given in the Laubach Way to Reading Teacher's Manual for Skill Book 3. Adapt the wording of the suggested teacher's instructions to the student as needed for your ESOL student's comprehension.

ADDITIONAL WRITTEN PRACTICE

After completing Lesson 5 in the skill book, have the student do the practices for Lesson 5 in the Workbook for Skill Book 3.

Lesson 6

<u>OBJECTIVES</u>

When a student completes this unit, he should be able to:

1. Say and respond to a new dialog.
2. Use some idioms with <u>take</u>, <u>do</u>, and <u>make</u>.
3. Say some vocabulary concerning items of personal grooming.
4. Use <u>by</u> + reflexive pronouns, as in <u>I</u> <u>live</u> <u>by</u> <u>myself</u>.
5. Use the past progressive tense.
6. Use infinitives and gerunds.
7. Listen to a story and repeat it in his own words.

<u>VISUAL AIDS</u>

1. <u>ESOL</u> <u>Illustrations</u> <u>3</u>, pp. 20-23.
2. Any of these items you can bring:

   washcloth   soap   toothbrush   shampoo   comb
   towel   razor   toothpaste   hairdryer   hairbrush

<u>I. Conversation Skills</u>

<u>DIALOG</u>

A: Where were you going when I saw you yesterday?
B: I was going to the movies.

A: Do you always go to the movies by yourself?
B: Sometimes I go alone, and sometimes I go with friends.

A: I'd like to go with you sometime.
B: That's a good idea. I'll call you.

VOCABULARY: Idioms with do, make, and take

---

do   make

Jason always does a good job.   Ray makes a good cup of coffee.
Jason does the dishes.   David makes good cakes.
Gail does the laundry.   Carla makes dinner for Rosa and herself.

take

I take a walk every day.
I take a shower or a bath every morning.
I take my lunch to work every day.

Model the sentences, asking the student to listen to does, makes, and take.
Use ESOL Illustrations 3, p. 20, for shower and bath, which are new here.

Note: These are idiomatic expressions which the student must learn.

DRILL: Making Sentences

Teacher gives the student a word or phrase which student uses in a sentence
with do, make, or take.

Teacher   Student

a good job
Jason always does a good job.   Jason always does a good job.

a walk
I take a walk every night.   I take a walk every night.

a shower in the morning
the dishes
my lunch to work
breakfast before I go to work
good cakes
a cup of coffee
a walk every morning
a bath in the evening

VOCABULARY: Items of Personal Grooming

I wash my hands with soap.
I wash my face with a washcloth.
I dry my hands and face with a towel.
I brush my teeth with a toothbrush and toothpaste.
I shave with a razor.
I wash my hair with shampoo.
I dry my hair with a hairdryer.
I comb my hair with a comb.
I brush my hair with a hairbrush.

Use actual objects or ESOL Illustrations 3, pp. 21-23.

DRILL: Question and Answer Drill

Teacher asks questions to elicit vocabulary items.

Teacher   Student

How do you brush your hair?
With a hairbrush.   With a hairbrush.

How do you comb your hair?
With a comb.   With a comb.

How do you wash your hands?
How do you dry your face?
How do you brush your teeth?
How do you shave?
How do you wash your hair?
How do you dry your hair?
How do you brush your hair?
How do you comb your hair?

STRUCTURE FOCUS: <u>by</u> + <u>Reflexive Pronouns</u>

    Do you live alone?   Yes, I live <u>by myself</u>.
    Does Jane live alone?   Yes, she lives <u>by herself</u>.
    Does David go to work alone? Yes, he goes <u>by himself</u>.

As you model the sentences, ask the student to listen to <u>by myself</u>, <u>by herself</u>, and <u>by himself</u>.

DRILL: Answering Questions

Teacher asks questions using the word <u>alone</u>.
Student answers using <u>by</u> and a reflexive pronoun. Student replies may vary.

<u>Teacher</u>   <u>Student</u>

Does Jane live alone?
Yes, she lives by herself.   Yes, she lives by herself.

Do you like to go shopping alone?
No, I don't like to go by myself. No, I don't like to go by myself.

Do you live alone?
Does Ann like to go shopping alone?
Do you go to class alone?
Do they go swimming alone?
Does David like to go to the movies alone?
Do you go fishing alone?

STRUCTURE FOCUS: <u>Past Progressive Tense</u>

He <u>was</u> <u>sleeping</u> when I called him last night.
I <u>was</u> <u>reading</u> a book when they called yesterday.
We <u>were</u> <u>watching</u> TV when you called.

As you model the sentences, ask the student to listen to <u>was</u> <u>sleeping</u>, <u>was</u> <u>reading</u>, and <u>were</u> <u>watching</u>.

<u>Note</u>: The past progressive tense is used for an action in progress at a particular time in the past.

DRILL: <u>Answering Questions</u>

Teacher asks questions which the student answers using the past progressive tense.

<u>Teacher</u>	<u>Student</u>

What was Lee doing
   when you called him last night?
sleeping
   He was sleeping
   when I called him last night.
	He was sleeping
	when I called him last night.

What was Jane reading
   when you called her yesterday?
a book
   She was reading a book
   when I called her yesterday.
	She was reading a book
	when I called her yesterday.

<u>Teacher</u>

What were you doing when they called yesterday?
studying

What was she doing when Rosa went to sleep?
singing to Rosa

What were you doing when you had the accident?
driving my car

What was she wearing when you saw her?
a red dress

What was Lee doing when you called him?
eating dinner

STRUCTURE FOCUS: Review of Infinitive and Gerund

I'll learn   to speak English in this class.
I'll tell him to read the book.

I'll finish   reading the book.
He has quit   working.

As you model the sentences, ask the student to listen to to speak, to read, reading, and working.

DRILL: Completion Drill

Teacher begins a sentence which student completes with either to do it or doing it.

Teacher   Student

I'll wait
I'll wait to do it.   I'll wait to do it.

I have finished
I have finished doing it.   I have finished doing it.

Teacher

| I'll learn | I'll need | I'll plan | I'll wait | She'll stop |
| I'll keep | I'll quit | I'll remember | He'll practice | They'll finish |

LISTENING COMPREHENSION

Many people have cameras. They take pictures of their family and their friends. They take pictures of trees and rivers. They put the pictures in a book. Then they show the pictures to their family and friends.

---

1. Teacher reads the story twice at a normal pace.
   Student listens. Student asks about words he does not know.

2. Student tells the story in his own words. If the student cannot tell the story, teacher may begin the sentence and have the student complete it.

Note: If the student cannot remember the story, read it once or twice again.

ORAL EVALUATION

1. Using ESOL Illustrations 3, p. 20, review idioms with do, make, and take by doing the drill on Making Sentences. Student should know all the idioms.

2. Using ESOL Illustrations 3, pp. 21-23, review items of personal grooming. Students should know 7 of them.

3. Review the use of by + reflexive pronouns by doing the Answering Questions Drill.

4. Review the past progressive tense by doing the Answering Questions Drill.

5. Review the use of the infinitive and the gerund by doing the Completion Drill.

II. Reading and Writing

SKILL BOOK 3: Lesson 6

Complete Lesson 6 in Skill Book 3, following the instructions given in the Laubach Way to Reading Teacher's Manual for Skill Book 3. Adapt the wording of the suggested teacher's instructions to the student as needed for your ESOL student's comprehension.

ADDITIONAL WRITTEN PRACTICE

After completing Lesson 6 in the skill book, have the student do the practices for Lesson 6 in the Workbook for Skill Book 3.

Lesson 7

When a student completes this unit, he should be able to:

1. Say and respond to a new dialog.
2. Say some words about beverages.
3. Say some words concerning the outdoors.
4. Say some adjectives about feelings.
5. Say some adjectives that are opposites.
6. Say some vocabulary about the inside of a car.
7. Use the word <u>again</u>.
8. Use the irregular verbs <u>sleep</u>, <u>keep</u>, <u>feel</u>, <u>sweep</u>, <u>mean</u>, <u>send</u>, <u>spend</u>
   and their past participles.
9. Use <u>am</u>, <u>is</u>, <u>are</u>, <u>was</u>, and <u>were</u> for emphasis.
10. Use <u>do</u>, <u>does</u>, and <u>did</u> for emphasis.
11. Listen to numbers and write them down.

VISUAL AIDS

1. <u>ESOL</u> <u>Illustrations</u> <u>3</u>, pp. 24-26.
2. Some ads for used cars from the newspaper.

I. Conversation Skills

DIALOG

       A: I'd like to buy a car.
       B: Cars are expensive. What kind are you going to get?

       A: A small used car. One that gets good gas mileage.
       B: That's a good idea.
          Maybe you'll find some ads for used cars in today's newspaper.
          Let's look.

       A: OK.

Use <u>ESOL</u> <u>Illustrations</u> <u>3</u>, p. 24.
Also, show some used car ads from the newspaper.

VOCABULARY: Beverages

When it's hot, a person likes to have a cold drink.
Some people drink water or soda with ice in it.
Some people drink iced tea or iced coffee.
Some people drink cold beer.
Some people drink wine.

Use ESOL Illustrations 3, p. 25.

DRILL: Identification Drill

Teacher asks a question (such as "What do some people drink when it's hot?"),
pointing to the illustrations on p. 25 of ESOL Illustrations 3.

Note: Review all previous words after each new word.

DRILL: Answering Questions

Teacher asks questions which elicit vocabulary items about beverages.
Student must give a different answer each time.

Teacher	Student
What do some people like to drink?	
iced tea	
Some people like to drink iced tea.	Some people like to drink iced tea.
What do you like to drink?	
etc.	

VOCABULARY: The Outdoors

I like to go camping.
I like to be outdoors.
I like the green trees and the blue sky.
I like the fresh air.

Use ESOL Illustrations 3, p. 24. You can color the trees green and the sky blue before class.

DRILL: Identification

Teacher asks a question about the vocabulary having to do with the outdoors, pointing to the appropriate illustration on p. 24 of ESOL Illustrations 3.

Note: Review all previous words after each new word.

VOCABULARY: Adjectives about Feelings

We feel angry when a friend yells at us.
We feel sad when a friend is sick.
We feel glad when a friend gets better.
Mrs. Green feels upset when her son comes home very late.

Pantomime the meaning of the adjectives.

DRILL: Question and Answer Drill

Teacher asks questions to elicit vocabulary items.

Teacher	Student
How do we feel when a friend yells at us? We feel angry.	We feel angry.
How do we feel when a friend is sick? We feel sad.	We feel sad.

How do we feel when a friend gets better?
How do we feel when a friend yells at us?
How do we feel when a friend is sick?
How does Mrs. Green feel when her son comes home late?

VOCABULARY: Adjective Opposites

The book is open.
The book is shut.

Beans are cheap.
Meat is expensive.

The day is bright.
The night is dark.

The big building is high.
The small building is low.

He's working in the garden. His hands are dirty.
He washes his hands. His hands are clean.

---

1. Teacher models each word in pairs of sentences, giving the opposites. Explain the words the student doesn't understand. Student listens.

2. Teacher models the pairs of sentences. Student repeats each pair of sentences.

DRILL: Question and Answer Drill

Teacher asks student to give vocabulary items.

Teacher	Student
Tell about the book.
The book is open.	The book is open.
Tell about beans.
Beans are cheap.	Beans are cheap.

Tell about meat.
Tell about beans.
Tell about the day.
Tell about the night.
Tell about the big building.
Tell about the small building.
Tell about the book. (Open the book.)
Tell about the book. (Shut the book.)
Tell about your hands when you wash them.
Tell about your hands when you work in the garden.

VOCABULARY: Inside the Car

Inside the car there is a steering wheel.
There is a front seat and a back seat.
The driver sits on the front seat behind the wheel.
The passenger sits on the passenger's side in the front seat.
Passengers sit in the back seat.

Use ESOL Illustrations 3, p. 26.

DRILL: Question and Answer Drill

Teacher asks questions to elicit vocabulary items.

Teacher   Student

Where does the driver sit?
The driver sits in the front seat   The driver sits in the front seat
   behind the wheel.   behind the wheel.

Where does the passenger sit?
The passenger sits   The passenger sits
   on the passenger's side   on the passenger's side
   in the front seat.   in the front seat.

Who sits in the back seat?
Where is the steering wheel?
Where does the driver sit?
Where do the passengers sit?

VOCABULARY: The Use of <u>again</u>

           The plate isn't clean. Wash it <u>again</u>.
           I didn't understand the story. Read it <u>again</u>.

As you model each pair of sentences, ask the student to listen to <u>again</u>.

DRILL: <u>Rejoinder Drill</u>

Teacher makes a statement, to which the student replies using the imperative and
<u>again</u>.

Teacher	Student
The plates aren't clean. Wash them again.	Wash them again.
I don't understand this story. Read it again.	Read it again.
The cups are still dirty. The knives are still dirty. I can't say this word. I don't understand this story.	

VOCABULARY: <u>Irregular Verbs</u>

         I <u>sleep</u> very well at night.
         I <u>feel</u> fine.
         He <u>keeps</u> his wallet in his pocket.
         I <u>sweep</u> the floor every day.
         He <u>means</u> a lot to me.
         I <u>send</u> my mother a letter every week.
         I <u>spend</u> a lot of money every week.

Pantomime the meaning of the verbs if an explanation is necessary.

VOCABULARY: <u>Past Participles of Irregular Verbs</u>

sleep	slept	have slept
keep	kept	have kept
feel	felt	have felt
sweep	swept	have swept
mean	meant	have meant
send	sent	have sent
spend	spent	have spent

Teacher models all three forms of each verb. Student repeats.

DRILL: <u>Answering Questions</u>

1. Teacher asks a question in the present perfect tense which the student answers in the negative.

2. Teacher models first two items. Student listens.

<u>Teacher</u>

Have you slept well this week?
No, I haven't slept well this week.

Have you kept on working?
No, I haven't kept on working.

Have you felt well this week?
Have you swept the floor yet?
Have you ever slept in a tent?
Have you meant what you said?
Have you sent Jane a letter yet?
Have you spent all your money yet?

<u>Student</u>

No, I haven't slept well this week.

No, I haven't kept on working.

STRUCTURE FOCUS: The Use of am, is, are for Emphasis

```
You aren't Spanish.      Yes, I am Spanish.
   He isn't married.     Yes, he is married.
   They aren't home.     Yes, they are home.

        It wasn't fun.   Yes, it was fun.
     She wasn't in bed.  Yes, she was in bed.
They weren't in the kitchen.  Yes, they were in the kitchen.
```

1. Teacher models the negative sentence and the emphatic sentence in pairs. Have the student listen to the emphatic form of the verb. Student listens.

2. Teacher models the sentences, stressing the verb be (am, is, are, was, were). Student repeats, also stressing the verb.

Note: The forms of the verb be are stressed in a sentence to emphasize the point being made and often to contradict something that has been said.

Drill: Rejoinder Drill

Teacher makes a statement in the negative which student contradicts by making an affirmative statement, stressing the verb be.

Teacher   Student

You aren't Cuban.
Yes, I am Cuban.   Yes, I am Cuban.

Ray isn't married to Kay.
Yes, he is married to Kay.   Yes, he is married to Kay.

Rosa isn't a baby.
They aren't home.
It wasn't fun.
The baby-sitter wasn't taking care of Rosa.
Kay isn't paying her bills.
They weren't playing basketball.

Structure Focus: The Use of do for Emphasis

You don't study English.	Yes, I do study English.
You don't live in _____.	Yes, I do live in _____.
He doesn't speak English.	Yes, he does speak English.
You didn't come to class last week.	Yes, I did come to class last week.
Kay didn't pay the rent.	Yes, Kay did pay the rent.
Ray didn't bake the cake.	Yes, Ray did bake the cake.

---

1. Teacher models the negative sentence and the emphatic affirmative sentence in pairs. Have the student listen to the emphatic form of the verb.

2. Teacher models each pair of sentences, stressing the verb do in the emphatic sentence. Student repeats the emphatic sentence, also stressing the verb.

Note: The verb do is used for emphasis. Be sure the student stresses do and did as he imitates the teacher.

DRILL: Rejoinder Drill

1. Teacher makes a statement in the negative which student contradicts by making an affirmative sentence using do or did.

2. Teacher models first two items. Student listens.

Teacher	Student
You don't study English.	
Yes, I do study English.	Yes, I do study English.
Ray didn't bake the cake.	
Yes, Ray did bake the cake.	Yes, Ray did bake the cake.
You don't live on _____ Street.	
Jason didn't fix the stairs.	
You don't study English.	
Kay and Ray didn't go away.	
They don't like to go camping.	
Kay didn't pay her bills.	
You didn't come to class yesterday.	

PRONUNCIATION AND LISTENING COMPREHENSION

1. Teacher says the numbers from 1 to 100 in groups of 10. Student listens.

2. Teacher models the numbers in groups of 10. Student repeats. Help the student with numbers he has difficulty with, such as the difference between 13 and 30, 14 and 40 and so on.

<u>DRILL</u>: Listening Comprehension

Teacher says the number. The student writes the number he hears on a piece of paper on the blackboard. Do not emphasize the endings (-<u>ty</u>, -<u>teen</u>). Read the numbers across, that is 3--13--30 and so on.

3	13	30
4	14	40
5	15	50
6	16	60
7	17	70
8	18	80
9	19	90

Do the numbers again in a different order; for example, say 13--6--9 and so on.

<u>ORAL EVALUATION</u>

1. Using <u>ESOL Illustrations 3</u>, p. 25, have the student identify the beverages. He should know 3 of them.

2. Using <u>ESOL Illustrations 3</u>, p. 24, have the student review terms about the outdoors. He should know all of them.

3. Review adjectives about feelings by doing the Question and Answer Drill. Student should know all of them.

4. Review adjective opposites by doing the Question and Answer Drill. Student should know all of them.

5. Review terms about inside the car by doing the Question and Answer Drill. Student should know all of them.

6. Review irregular verbs by doing the drill on Answering Questions. Student should know all of them.

7. Review <u>am</u>, <u>is</u>, <u>are</u> for emphasis by doing the Rejoinder Drill.

8. Review <u>do</u> for emphasis by doing the Rejoinder Drill.

<u>II. Reading and Writing</u>

<u>SKILL BOOK 3</u>: Lesson 7

Complete Lesson 7 in <u>Skill Book 3</u>, following the instructions given in the Laubach Way to Reading <u>Teacher's Manual for Skill Book 3</u>. Adapt the wording of the suggested teacher's instructions to the student as needed for your ESOL student's comprehension.

<u>ADDITIONAL WRITTEN PRACTICE</u>

After Completing Lesson 7 in the skill book, have the student do the practices for Lesson 7 in the <u>Workbook for Skill Book 3</u>.

Lesson 8

<u>OBJECTIVES</u>

When a student completes this unit, he should be able to:

1. Say and respond to a new dialog.
2. Say some prepositions.
3. Say some names of fruit.
4. Use indefinite pronouns: <u>everything</u>, <u>something</u>, <u>nothing</u>, <u>anything</u>.
5. Use indefinite pronouns: <u>everyone</u>, <u>someone</u>, <u>no one</u>, <u>anyone</u>.
6. Use <u>each</u>.
7. Use <u>best</u> and <u>worst</u> with the present prefect tense.
8. Listen to a story and repeat it in his own words.

<u>VISUAL AIDS</u>

1. <u>ESOL</u> <u>Illustrations</u> <u>3</u>, pp. 27-29.
2. Any of the following fruits that it is convenient to bring, or color pictures of them.

apple	bananas	grapes	lemon
pear	orange	peach	watermelon

I. Conversation Skills

<u>DIALOG</u>

A: Food is getting more expensive every day.
B: That's true.
   I can't afford to buy meat very often.

A: I know. We can't either.
   We eat a lot of beans and rice.
B: We do, too.

---

1. Model the entire dialog two or three times. Student listens.
2. Model each line. Student repeats after each line.
3. Teacher takes one role of the dialog. Student takes the other.
4. Reverse roles.

VOCABULARY: <u>Prepositions of Location</u>

Ray is sitting <u>between</u> Kay and Carla.
Carla is sitting <u>next to</u> Ray.
David is sitting <u>in back of</u> Carla.
Jason is sitting <u>in front of</u> Carla.
The teacher is <u>in the front of</u> the room.
The coats are <u>in the back of</u> the room.

Use <u>ESOL Illustrations 3</u>, p. 27, to show the meaning of each preposition.

DRILL: <u>Answering Questions</u>

Depending on the number of people in the room, the teacher can move around, placing herself <u>between</u> two students, <u>next to</u> a student, <u>in back of</u> one and <u>in front of</u> one. She may stand <u>in the front of</u> the room and <u>in the back of</u> the room. As the teacher stands in different positions, she asks questions like "Who am I standing between?" and "Where am I?" to elicit the prepositions being taught.

VOCABULARY: <u>Fruit</u>

Many people eat <u>fruit</u>.
They eat <u>apples</u>.
They eat <u>pears</u>.
They eat <u>bananas</u>.
They eat <u>oranges</u>.
They eat <u>grapes</u>.
They eat <u>watermelons</u>.
They eat <u>peaches</u>.
They eat <u>lemons</u>.

Use <u>ESOL Illustrations 3</u>, pp. 28-29, or actual objects, or color pictures of fruit.

<u>Note</u>: You may wish to add other fruits, depending on what foods are part of your student's diet, for example, pineapple, grapefruit, or cherries.

DRILL: <u>Identification Drill</u>

Teacher points to the illustrations on pp. 28-29 of <u>ESOL Illustrations 3</u> and asks, "What do people eat?"

STRUCTURE FOCUS: Indefinite Pronouns with -thing

Everything is on the table.
Something is on the table.
Nothing is on the table.
There isn't anything on the table.

As you model each sentence, ask the student to listen to everything, something, nothing, and anything.

Note: The words everything, something, nothing, and anything are indefinite pronouns. They take a singular verb.

DRILL: Making Sentences

Teacher uses one indefinite pronoun in a sentence and asks the student to substitute the other indefinite pronouns in the same sentence or a similar one.

Teacher	Student
Everything is here.	
nothing	
Nothing is here.	Nothing is here.
anything	
There isn't anything here.	There isn't anything here.
Everything is on the desk.	
something	
nothing	
anything	
Everything looks nice.	
something	
nothing	
I see everything in the room.	
something	
nothing	
anything	

STRUCTURE FOCUS: Indefinite Pronouns with -one

Everyone is here.
Someone is here
No one is here.
There isn't anyone here.

As you model each sentence, ask the student to listen to everyone, someone, no one, and anyone. Explain that these words refer to persons.

Note: The words everyone, someone, no one, and anyone are indefinite pronouns that refer to a person or persons. They take a singular verb. In informal usage, we say "Everyone must hand in their papers." In formal usage, we say "Everyone must hand in his paper."

DRILL: Making Sentences

Teacher uses one indefinite pronoun in a sentence and asks the student to substitute the other indefinite pronouns in the same sentence or a similar one.

Teacher	Student
Everyone is in the room.	
someone	
Someone is in the room.	Someone is in the room.
no one	
No one is in the room.	No one is in the room.
anyone	
There isn't anyone in the room.	There isn't anyone in the room.

I see everyone in the room.
someone
no one
anyone

I will give everyone a gift.
someone
no one
anyone

Everyone knows the answer.
someone
no one

STRUCTURE FOCUS: The Use of each

Each book is the same.
Each person brings something to the party.

As you model each sentence, ask the student to listen to each.

Note: Each takes a singular verb.

DRILL: Making Sentences

Teacher makes a sentence about everyone in the class.
Student makes a similar sentence using each.

Teacher	Student
Everyone in the class has a book. each book Each book is the same.	Each book is the same.
Everyone in the class has a car. each car Each car is not the same.	Each car is not the same.
Everyone in the class has a name. each name	
Everyone in the class is wearing a ring. each ring	
Everyone in the class has a book. each book	
Everyone in the class has a camera. each camera	
Everyone in the class has a pen. each pen	

STRUCTURE FOCUS: The Present Perfect Tense with best and worst

---

This is the best sandwich I have ever eaten.
This is the best party we have ever had.
This is the worst music I have ever listened to.
This is the worst meat I have ever eaten.

As you model each sentence, ask the student to listen to the best or the worst.

Note: Explain that best is used for something very good, while worst is used for something very bad. (It is not necessary at this time to teach good, better, best and bad, worse, worst.)

DRILL: Completion Drill

Teacher begins a sentence containing best or worst, which the student completes using the present perfect tense.

Teacher   Student

This is the best sandwich
    This is the best sandwich   This is the best sandwich
    I have ever eaten.   I have ever eaten.

This is the worst cake.
    This is the worst cake   This is the worst cake
    I have ever eaten.   I have ever eaten.

This is the best party
This is the worst meat
You are the best friend
These are the worst beans
This is the best music

LISTENING COMPREHENSION

Carla's class had a dinner party. There were eighteen people at the party. They had meat, beans, baked potatoes, and a green salad. They had tea, coffee, apples, and cheese. They had fun eating a big meal together.

---

1. Teacher reads the story twice at a normal pace.
   Student listens. Student asks about words he does not know.

2. Student tells the story in his own words. If the student cannot tell the story, teacher may begin the sentence and have the student complete it.

Note: If the student cannot remember the story, read it once or twice again.

ORAL EVALUATION

1. Review prepositions of location by doing the drill on Answering Questions. Student should know all the prepositions.

2. Using ESOL Illustrations 3, pp. 28-29, have the student identify the names of the fruits. Student should know 7 of them.

3. Review the indefinite pronouns with -thing and -one by doing the two drills on Making Sentences.

4. Review each by doing the drill on Making Sentences.

5. Review the use of best and worst with the present perfect tense by doing the Completion Drill.

II. Reading and Writing

SKILL BOOK 3: Lesson 8

Complete Lesson 8 in Skill Book 3, following the instructions given in the Laubach Way to Reading Teacher's Manual for Skill Book 3. Adapt the wording of the suggested teacher's instructions to the student as necessary for the comprehension of your ESOL student.

ADDITIONAL WRITTEN PRACTICE

After completing Lesson 8 in the skill book, have the student do the practices for Lesson 8 in the Workbook for Skill Book 3.

Lesson 9

OBJECTIVES

When a student completes this unit, he should be able to:

1. Say and respond to a new dialog.
2. Say words concerning a repair bill: repair, parts, labor, tax.
3. Say some words concerning items used for cleaning.
4. Say the chart word key.
5. Say some words about saving money.
6. Say the ordinal numbers: first to one hundredth.
7. Use the past be + going to.
8. Use adjective clauses with that.
9. Listen to a story and repeat it in his own words.

VISUAL AIDS

1. ESOL Illustrations 3, pp. 30-31.
2. Keys on a chain.

I. Conversation Skills

DIALOG

| | Steve: | May I help you? |
| Mrs. Green: | Yes, I'd like to have my radio fixed. |

| | Steve: | What's wrong with it? |
| Mrs. Green: | I don't know. It doesn't work. |

| | Steve: | We'll look it over and try to fix it. |
| Mrs. Green: | When will it be ready? |

| | Steve: | In a week. Here's your ticket for the radio. |
| Mrs. Green: | Thank you. |

Vary the dialog by practicing with other items to be repaired that the student may suggest.

VOCABULARY: A Repair Bill

Jane Fisher's TV was not working.
She asked Pete to fix her TV. Pete has a repair shop.
Jane's TV repair cost $12.14 for new parts.
Her TV repair cost $30.00 for the labor Peter did to fix the TV.
The sales tax on her bill was $2.53.

Note: Explain that repair means "fix" and that parts for a TV could be a new knob or picture tube. "Labor" is the work involved. Discuss the local sales tax student must pay in his community.

DRILL: Answering Questions

Teacher asks questions to elicit vocabulary items.

Teacher	Student
Was Jane Fisher's TV working?	
No, her TV wasn't working.	No, her TV wasn't working.
Why did she ask Pete to fix her TV?	
Pete had a repair shop.	Pete had a repair shop.
What did Jane pay $12.14 for?	
What did Jane pay $30.00 for?	
What did Jane pay $2.53 for?	
How much is the sales tax where you live?	

VOCABULARY: Items Used for Cleaning

When Steve cleans the shop, he uses many things.
He sweeps the floor with a broom.
He picks up the dirt with a dustpan.
He washes the floor with a mop.
He vacuums the rug with a vacuum cleaner.
He puts soap and water in a pail and washes the windows with a sponge.
He puts old paper and dirt in a trash can.

Use ESOL Illustrations 3, pp. 30-31.

DRILL: Question and Answer Drill

Teacher asks questions to elicit vocabulary items.

Teacher	Student
What does Steve sweep the floor with?	
A broom.	A broom.
What does he pick the dirt up with?	
A dustpan.	A dustpan.

What does Steve wash the floor with?
What does he sweep the floor with?
What does he vacuum the rug with?
Where does he put soap and water?
Where does he put the old paper and dirt?
What does he pick the dirt up with?

VOCABULARY: Kinds of Keys

I have a lot of keys.
I keep my keys on a key chain.
I have a house key.
I have a car key.
I have a key to my bicycle lock.

VOCABULARY: Saving Money

Every week I spend money on food and rent.
Every week I save some money.
I save the money in the bank.
I put my money in a savings account.
I want to save money to buy many things.

VOCABULARY: Ordinal Numbers

first	eleventh	tenth
second	twelfth	twentieth
third	thirteenth	thirtieth
fourth	fourteenth	fortieth
fifth	fifteenth	fiftieth
sixth	sixteenth	sixtieth
seventh	seventeenth	seventieth
eighth	eighteenth	eightieth
ninth	nineteenth	nintieth
tenth	twentieth	one hundredth

1. Teacher models the ordinal numbers in groups of five, going down each column here. (In the last column, when you are counting by 10s, start again at tenth.)

2. Teacher models the numbers. Student repeats after each number.

DRILL: Saying Ordinal Numbers

1. Teacher writes a number on the board and says the number. Student repeats.

2. Teacher writes a number on the board. Student says the number.

3. Reverse roles. Have the student say the numbers as the teacher writes the numbers on the board.

Note: Help the student with his pronunciation if necessary.

VOCABULARY: <u>Using Ordinal Numbers in Sentences</u>

```
_____

                We went to Snake River for three days.
                The first day we went swimming.
                The second day we went fishing.
                The third day we had a picnic.
_____
```

1. Teacher models each number in a sentence. Student listens.
2. Teacher models the sentences. Student repeats after each sentence.

DRILL: <u>Answering Questions</u>

Teacher asks questions which elicit the ordinal numbers in the student's answers.

<u>Teacher</u>   <u>Student</u>

When did you go swimming at Snake River?
We went swimming the first day.   We went swimming the first day.

When did you go fishing at Snake River?
We went fishing the second day.   We went fishing the second day.

When did you go swimming at Snake River?
When did you go fishing at Snake River?
When did you go on a picnic at Snake River?
What is the first thing you do when you come to class?
What is the first thing you do when you get up in the morning?

STRUCTURE FOCUS: Past of be + going to

I was going to buy the watch, but I didn't.
We were going to go home at 7 o'clock, but we didn't.
They were going to buy a car, but they didn't.

As you model each sentence, ask the student to listen to was going to and
were going to.

Note: The form be in the past + going to is used to express a past intention
that may not have been carried out.

DRILL: Answering Questions

Teacher asks questions which student answers using the past of
be + going + infinitive.

Teacher   Student

What were you going to do before class?
I was going to study but I didn't.   I was going to study but I didn't.

What was Jason going to do first?
He was going to paint the stairs first.   He was going to paint the stairs first.

What was Carla going to bake?
Which bill was Kay going to pay?
What were you going to buy?
Where were you going to go after class?
When were you going to have a party?
What was Pete going to do?

STRUCTURE FOCUS: Adjective Clauses with that

Steve gave Mrs. Green the radio that he fixed.
I like the frame that Gail put her picture in.
You can keep the money that Mrs. Green gave you.

As you model each sentence, ask the student to listen to that.

DRILL: Combining Sentences

Teacher gives two sentences which the student combines using an adjective clause with that.

Teacher   Student

Steve gave Mrs. Green the radio.
He fixed the radio.
    Steve gave Mrs. Green the radio   Steve gave Mrs. Green the radio
    that he fixed.   that he fixed.

I like the frame.
Gail put her picture in the frame.
    I like the frame   I like the frame
    that Gail put her picture in.   that Gail put her picture in.

You can keep the money.
Mrs. Green gave you the money.

Mrs. Smith brings the meat.
Each person helped to pay for the meat.

They painted the apartment.
They live in the apartment.

Mrs. King is a lady.
I like her a lot.

They cut the wedding cake.
Jason's mother baked the cake.

Lee Green went to see the tree.
He hit the tree.

At the party they had the beans.
Carla made the beans.

LISTENING COMPREHENSION

I was going to listen to my radio, but it wasn't working. I took the radio to the Valley Repair Shop. I asked Pete to fix my radio. He said he was very busy. He needed a week to fix my radio. I was sorry. I need my radio. I listen to music and the news on the radio every morning and every night.

---

1. Teacher reads the story twice at a normal pace. Student listens. Student asks about words he does not know.

2. Student tells the story in his own words. If the student cannot tell the story, teacher may begin the sentence and have the student complete it.

Note: If the student cannot remember the story, read it once or twice again.

ORAL EVALUATION

1. Review the words concerning a repair bill by doing the drill on Answering Questions. Student should know all the items.

2. Using ESOL Illustrations 3, pp. 30-31, review words on items used for cleaning by doing the Question and Answer Drill. Student should know 5 of the items.

3. Review words about saving money. Student should know all the words.

4. Review the ordinal numbers by doing the drill on Saying Ordinal Numbers.

5. Review the past of be + going to by doing the drill on Answering Questions.

6. Review adjective clauses with that by doing the drill on Combining Sentences.

II. Reading and Writing

SKILL BOOK 3: Lesson 9

Complete Lesson 9 in Skill Book 3, following the instructions given in the Laubach Way to Reading Teacher's Manual for Skill Book 3. Adapt the wording of the suggested teacher's instructions to the student as necessary for the comprehension of your ESOL student.

ADDITIONAL WRITTEN PRACTICE

After completing Lesson 9 in the skill book, have the student do the practices for Lesson 9 in the Workbook for Skill Book 3.

Lesson 10

<u>OBJECTIVES</u>

When a student completes this unit, he should be able to:

1. Say and respond to a new dialog.
2. Say some words about the stages of life.
3. Say some story words: <u>Canada</u>, <u>the United States</u>, <u>country</u>, <u>city</u>, and <u>state</u>.
4. Use some idioms with <u>take</u> and <u>make</u>.
5. Use <u>more...than</u> with nouns.
6. Use question words + infinitives.
7. Listen to a story and repeat it in his own words.

<u>VISUAL AIDS</u>

<u>ESOL Illustrations 3</u>, pp. 32-33.

I. Conversation Skills

<u>DIALOG</u>

A: I really like your new car.
B: Thanks. I do, too.

A: When did you get it?
B: About three weeks ago.

A: How does it run?
B: Great. It's a nice car.

<u>VOCABULARY</u>: <u>Stages of Life</u>

An <u>infant</u> is a baby.
A <u>child</u> is a very young person.
A <u>teenager</u> is anyone from the age of 13 to 19.
An <u>adult</u> is anyone over 21 years old.

Use <u>ESOL Illustrations 3</u>, p. 32.

<u>DRILL</u>: <u>Identification Drill</u>

Teacher asks "Who's this?" as she points to the various people on p. 32 of <u>ESOL Illustrations 3</u>.

VOCABULARY: Canada and the United States

Canada and the United States are big countries.
Canada is a neighbor of the United States.
The United States has fifty states.
It has many, many cities.
Ann Baker lives in the city of Dallas, in the state of Texas.

---

1. Use ESOL Illustrations 3, p. 33. On that map, write in the names of the student's city and state. Point out other cities and states the student knows or is interested in. Student listens.

2. Teacher models the sentences. Student repeats after each sentence.

DRILL: Question and Answer Drill

Teacher asks questions to elicit vocabulary items.

Teacher	Student
What are Canada and the United States?	
They are big countries.	They are big countries.
How many states does the United States have?	
The United States has 50 states.	The United States has 50 states.

What is Canada?
How many cities does the United States have?
What country is a neighbor of the United States?
Where does Ann Baker live?
What city do you live in?
What state do you live in?

VOCABULARY: Idioms with take and make

I take a bus to work every morning.
I take a break at 10 o'clock.
I take English at school.
I take some medicine when I am sick.

I made an appointment with the doctor for a checkup.
I made a date with my friend to go to the movies.
I made a mistake and got on the wrong bus.
I made a mess when I dropped the food.

As you model the sentences, have the student listen to take and made.

Explain any of the idioms the student does not understand. For example, take a break means to stop working for a short time. Make an appointment is used for business, whereas make a date is used for social occasions.

DRILL: Making Sentences

Teacher gives the student a word or phrase which the student uses in a sentence with take or make(made).

Teacher	Student
a bus
I take a bus to work every morning.	I take a bus to work every morning.
a mistake
I made a mistake when I added the numbers.	I made a mistake when I added the numbers.

Teacher

a break	a date	English	a bus
an appointment	some medicine	a mess	

STRUCTURE FOCUS: <u>more</u>...<u>than</u> with Nouns

She has three books
I have two books.
She has <u>more</u> books <u>than</u> I do.

David has three pencils.
Ed has one pencil.
David has <u>more</u> pencils <u>than</u> Ed does.

---

1. Teacher models each set of three sentences, asking the student to listen to <u>more</u>...<u>than</u>. Student listens.

2. Teacher models each set of three sentences. Student repeats the sentence with <u>more</u>...<u>than</u>.

<u>Note</u>: In these sentences <u>more</u> is used with nouns. It indicates a greater number and is used to compare two of anything.

DRILL: <u>Combining Sentences</u>

Teacher gives two sentences which the student combines into one using <u>more</u>...<u>than</u>.

<u>Teacher</u>	<u>Student</u>
Ann has two dogs. Ed has one dog. Ann has more dogs than Ed does.	Ann has more dogs than Ed does.
She has four books. I have two books. She has more books than I do.	She has more books than I do.
We have three cats. They have two cats.	
She takes two buses to go to work. I take one bus to go to work.	
The Smiths have two cars. We have one car.	
The Smiths have three children. We have two children.	
Ann made three mistakes yesterday. Gail made two mistakes yesterday.	
I take two breaks at work every day. Ed takes one break at work every day.	

STRUCTURE FOCUS: Question Words + Infinitive

Please tell me	where	to put	these books.
I don't know	what	to do.	
Ann will teach you	how	to swim.	
He's learning	how	to play	hockey.

As you model each sentence, ask the student to listen to where, what, and how.

Note: The question words when, where, who, what, how may be followed by an infinitive.

DRILL: Completion Drill

Teacher gives the beginning of a sentence which the student completes using an infinitive.

Teacher

Kay will teach me how
Kay will teach me how to play cards.

I want to learn how
I want to learn how to read.

Please tell me what
I know where
She wants to know how many plates
Ann is going to teach me how
They know when

Student

Kay will teach me how to play cards.

I want to learn how to read.

LISTENING COMPREHENSION

Pete runs the repair shop on Second Street. He fixes radios, TVs, and many other things. He makes money fixing things. But he really likes to teach hockey. He teaches teenagers to play hockey. They are having fun learning the game. They want to be the best hockey team in the valley.
---

1. Teacher reads the story twice at a normal pace.
   Student listens. Student asks about words he does not know.

2. Student tells the story in his own words. If the student cannot tell the story, teacher may begin the sentence and have the student complete it.

Note: If the student cannot remember the story, read it once or twice again.

ORAL EVALUATION

1. Using ESOL Illustrations 3, p. 32, review the stages of life by identifying the illustrations. Student should know all the words.

2. Using ESOL Illustrations 3, p. 33, review the words about Canada and the United States. Student should know all the words.

3. Review idioms take and make by doing the drill on Making Sentences. Student should know 6 of the idioms.

4. Review the use of more...than with nouns by doing the drill on Combining Sentences.

5. Review the use of question words + infinitives by doing the Completion Drill.

II. Reading and Writing

SKILL BOOK 3: Lesson 10

Complete Lesson 10 in Skill Book 3, following the instructions given in the Laubach Way to Reading Teacher's Manual for Skill Book 3. Adapt the wording of the suggested teacher's instructions to the student as necessary for your ESOL student's comprehension.

ADDITIONAL WRITTEN PRACTICE

After completing Lesson 10 in the skill book, have the student do the practices for Lesson 10 in the Workbook for Skill Book 3.

Lesson 11

OBJECTIVES

When a student completes this unit, he should be able to:

1. Say and respond to a new dialog.
2. Say some words about date of birth.
3. Say some words about getting a driver's license.
4. Say some terms on an application.
5. Use simple if clauses.
6. Use must and must not.
7. Listen to a story and repeat it in his own words.

VISUAL AIDS

1. ESOL Illustrations 3, pp. 34-35.
2. A driver's license.
3. An application for a driver's license, if it is possible to obtain one from your state.

I. Conversation Skills

DIALOG

_____

A: Can I help you fill out your application?
B: Would you, please? I don't understand it.

A: What's the problem?
B: What does M or F mean?

A: M is for male, a man.
   F is for female, a woman.
B: Oh, I see. That's easy.
   What is a zip code?

A: It's the number the post office gives your state, city, and street. It's part of your address.

_____

VOCABULARY: Date of Birth

Ed is 20 years old. What is his <u>age</u>? It's 20.
He <u>was</u> <u>born</u> in _____ (year).
The <u>date</u> <u>of</u> <u>his</u> <u>birth</u> is January 1, 19___.
His <u>birthday</u> is on January 1.

Fill in the year of birth that will be accurate for a 20-year-old person.
Explain that it is not polite to ask a person what his age is.

DRILL: Answering Questions

Teacher asks questions to elicit the vocabulary.

Teacher	Student
How old is Ed?	
He is 20 years old.	He is 20 years old.
What is his age?	
He's 20.	He's 20.
When was Ed born?	
What is the date of Ed's birth?	
When is Ed's birthday?	
When is your birthday?	

VOCABULARY: Getting a Driver's License

Ed <u>rides</u> a <u>bicycle</u> to work.
He does not need a <u>license</u> to ride a bicycle.

David <u>drives</u> a car to work.
He needs a license to drive a car.
He needs <u>license</u> <u>plates</u> for his car.

You need to take a <u>written</u> <u>test</u> and
  a <u>driver's</u> <u>test</u> to get a driver's license.
The person who gives the test is a <u>tester</u>.

Use <u>ESOL</u> <u>Illustrations</u> <u>3</u>, pp. 34-35. Also show an actual driver's license.

DRILL: Identification Drill

Teacher asks the question "What's this?" or "Who's this?" to elicit the vocabulary items. Point to the appropriate picture on pp. 34-35 of <u>ESOL</u> <u>Illustrations</u> <u>3</u>.

VOCABULARY: Terms on an Application

To get a driver's license, you need to fill out an application.

You have to write your name and address.
Your address is the street you live on, the city, the state,
    and the post office zip code number.

You have to give your date of birth--the month, day, and year.
You have to give your sex--male or female.

Use an actual driver's license application or ESOL Illustrations 3, p. 35.
Explain the words the student does not understand: male is man, female is woman.

DRILL: Answering Questions

Teacher asks questions which elicit the vocabulary items. Help the student with
his personal information, but do not insist that he give his date of birth if he
prefers not to.

Teacher   Student

What do you need to fill out
to get a driver's license?
    You need to fill out an application.   You need to fill out an application.

What is a person's address?
    An address is a person's street,   An address is a person's street,
    city, state, and zip code.   city, state, and zip code.

What does date of birth mean?
What does male mean?
What does female mean?
What is your address?
What is your zip code?
What is your birthday?
Are you male or female?

STRUCTURE FOCUS: If Clauses

> _If_ you pass the driver's test,
>   you will get a driver's license.
>
> _If_ Ray and Kay have enough money,
>   they will go away for three days.

As you model each sentence, ask the student to listen to _if_.

Note: These _if_ clauses are true in the present or future time.
The simple present is used in the _if_ clause; the future tense with _will_
(or the present tense) is used in the main clause.

DRILL: Answering Questions

Teacher asks questions which elicit answers with _if_ clauses.
Student replies may vary.

Teacher	Student
If you pass the driver's test, what will you get?	
If I pass the driver's test, I'll get a license.	If I pass the driver's test, I'll get a license.
What will Kay and Ray do if they have enough money?	
If Kay and Ray have enough money, they will go away.	If Kay and Ray have enough money, they will go away.

What will you buy if you have enough money?
What will you do if you have enough time?
Where will you go if you have some money?
What will you get if you pass the driver's test?

STRUCTURE FOCUS: The Use of <u>must</u> and <u>must not</u>

```
            You must have a driver's license to drive a car.
            You must stop for a red light.

            You must not drive without a driver's license.
            A person must not touch a hot stove.
```

As you model each sentence, ask the student to listen to <u>must</u> and <u>must</u> <u>not</u>.

Note: In the affirmative, <u>must</u> is used to indicate strong obligation. In the negative, <u>must</u> <u>not</u> indicates that something is prohibited.

DRILL: Completion Drill

Teacher gives a phrase which the student uses in a sentence with <u>must</u> or <u>must</u> <u>not</u>.

Teacher	Student
stop for a red light You must stop for a red light.	You must stop for a red light.

drive without a driver's license
    You must not drive
    without a driver's license.
	You must not drive
	without a driver's license.

go through a red light
touch a hot stove
stop for a red light
take a driver's test to get a driver's license
put your hand in the fire
drive without a license
write in library books

LISTENING COMPREHENSION

       In many states, when you are 16, you can get a permit to
drive a car. With a permit, you can start driving, but a person
with a driver's license must ride with you. When you think you can
drive, you can take a driver's test. If you pass it, you can get a
driver's license. Then you can drive alone.

---

1. Teacher reads the story twice at a normal pace.
   Student listens. Student asks about words he does not know.

2. Student tells the story in his own words. If the student cannot tell the
   story, teacher may begin the sentence and have the student complete it.

Note: If the student cannot remember the story, read it once or twice again.

ORAL EVALUATION

1. Review vocabulary on date of birth by doing the drill on Answering Questions.
   Student should be able to answer all of the questions.

2. Using ESOL Illustrations 3, pp. 34-35, have the student say the words about
   getting a driver's license. Student should know all of them.

3. Using ESOL Illustrations 3, p. 35, review terms on an application by doing
   the drill on Answering Questions. Student should be able to answer all the
   questions.

4. Review if clauses by doing the drill on Answering Questions.

5. Review must and must not by doing the Completion Drill.

II. Reading and Writing

SKILL BOOK 3: Lesson 11

Complete Lesson 11 in Skill Book 3, following the instructions given in the
Laubach Way to Reading Teacher's Manual for Skill Book 3. Adapt the wording of
the suggested teacher's instructions to the student as needed for your ESOL
student's comprehension.

ADDITIONAL WRITTEN PRACTICE

After completing Lesson 11 in the skill book, have the student do the practices
for Lesson 11 in the Workbook for Skill Book 3.

Lesson 12

OBJECTIVES

When a student completes this unit, he should be able to:

1. Say and respond to a new dialog.
2. Say words concerning length: <u>inch</u>, <u>foot</u>, <u>yard</u>, and <u>mile</u>.
3. Say words concerning feelings: <u>smile</u>, <u>laugh</u>, <u>frown</u>, and <u>cry</u>.
4. Say words about running in a race.
5. Say words about being retired.
6. Distinguish between <u>signing</u> and <u>printing</u> one's name.
7. Say the words <u>for sale</u>, <u>salesperson</u>, and <u>price</u>.
8. Use <u>has/have been</u> + verb-<u>ing</u>.
9. Use <u>while</u> clauses.
10. Review short answers to questions.
11. Listen to a story and repeat it in his own words.

VISUAL AIDS

A ruler or tape measure. (You will need to show an inch, a foot, and a yard.)

I. Conversation Skills

DIALOG

A: Are you going to watch Fran run in the race?
B: I didn't know she was going to run.

A: Yes, she's been running every day for three years.
   She's a good runner.
B: I'd like to watch Fran run.
   When is the race?

A: Next Saturday.
   Let's go together.
B: OK.

VOCABULARY: Measures of Length

This is one inch.
There are 12 inches in a foot.
There are 3 feet in a yard.
There are 5,280 feet in one mile.

As you model the sentences, use a ruler or tape measure to show inch, foot, and yard.

Note: To give the student a better understanding of mile, you may also want to add a sentence (It is a mile from ____ to ____.), using two places that he would recognize. Also, it would be helpful to know in advance the distance from your student's home to class for the drill that follows.

DRILL: Question and Answer Drill

Teacher asks "How long is this?" to elicit vocabulary items.
Point to a measure on the ruler or tape measure.

Teacher	Student
How long is this?	
It's one inch.	It's one inch.
How long is this?	
It's one foot.	It's one foot.

Teacher (pointing to the ruler)

6 inches
3 feet
1 foot
1 yard

Teacher

How tall are you?
How far is it from your house to class?

VOCABULARY: Verbs That Express Feelings

When Fran is happy, she smiles.
When something is funny, Fran laughs.
When Fran is not happy, she frowns.
When Fran is very sad, she cries.
When Fran is angry, she shouts.

Act out the new verbs to show their meaning.

DRILL: Question and Answer Drill

Teacher asks questions to elicit vocabulary items.

Teacher	Student
What does Fran do when she's happy?	
She smiles.	She smiles.
What does Fran do when she is very sad?	
She cries.	She cries.

What does Fran do when something is funny?
What does Fran do when she's happy?
What does Fran do when she's not happy?
What does Fran do when she's very sad?
What does Fran do when she's angry?

VOCABULARY: Running in a Race

Fran is going to run in a race with 14 other women.
Fran wants to run fast.
She wants to win the race.
The winner will finish first.
There's a tie when two people finish at the same time.

VOCABULARY: A Retired Couple

Retired people have time to do things that they like.

Some people are very busy.
They don't have time to do the things they like.

Mike and Fran are over 62 and are retired.
They don't have jobs any more.
They have time to do the things that they like.

VOCABULARY: sign and print

When you write a letter, you sign your name.
You print your name on an application.

Demonstrate signing and printing your name on the blackboard or a piece of paper.

DRILL: Identification Drill

1. Sign your name while saying, "I am signing my name."
   Then print your name while saying, "I am printing my name."

2. Perform each action again, asking "What am I doing?"

VOCABULARY: For Sale

The things in stores are for sale.
Food is for sale at a supermarket.
Furniture is for sale at a furniture store.
Medicine is for sale at a drugstore.

A salesperson in a store sells things.
The money you pay for a thing is the price.

DRILL: Answering Questions

Teacher asks questions to elicit the vocabulary. The prices in student replies may vary.

Teacher	Student
What is the price of a newspaper?	
The price is 50 cents.	The price is 50 cents.
What is for sale at a drugstore?	
Medicine is for sale at a drugstore.	Medicine is for sale at a drugstore.

What does a salesperson do?
What is the price of a coat?
What is for sale at a supermarket?
What is for sale at a department store?
What is the price of a newspaper?
What is for sale at a furniture store?
What is for sale at a drugstore?
What does a salesperson do?

STRUCTURE FOCUS: have/has been + Verb-ing

```
        I'm tired. I   have been playing  hockey for three hours.
                Fran   has  been running  every day for three years.
               Jason   has  been going    to class for six months.
    Carla and David   have been studying  for two hours.
```

As you model each sentence, ask the student to listen to have been and has been.

Note: The present perfect progressive tense is used to describe an action that began in the past and continues in the present.

DRILL: Answering Questions

Teacher asks a question which the student answers using has been or have been + verb-ing.

Teacher   Student

How long have you been studying?
I have been studying for two hours.   I have been studying for two hours.

How long has Fran been running?
She has been running for three years.   She has been running for three years.

How long have you been sitting here?
How long has Jason been going to class?
How long have Carla and David been studying?
How long have you been reading that book?
How long has Steve been working on the radio?
How long has Pete been teaching the boys to play hockey?

STRUCTURE FOCUS: While Clauses

<u>While</u> his wife runs, Mike makes breakfast.
<u>While</u> Carla studies, David watches Rosa.
<u>While</u> I was walking, it started to rain.
<u>While</u> Ray was making a salad, Kay cooked the meat.

As you model each sentence, ask the student to listen to <u>while</u>.

<u>Note</u>: <u>While</u> is used when two actions occur at the same time in the present or past.

DRILL: Answering Questions

Teacher asks questions which the student answers using <u>while</u>.
Student replies may vary.

Teacher	Student
What does Mike do while his wife runs?	
Mike makes breakfast while his wife runs.	Mike makes breakfast while his wife runs.
What was Carla doing while the teacher talked?	
Carla was listening while the teacher talked.	Carla was listening while the teacher talked.

What were you doing while Carla studied?
What were you doing while Ann telephoned Gail?
What was Kay doing while Ray was making a salad?
What does the teacher do while you read?
What does Mike do while his wife runs?
What do you do while the teacher talks?

STRUCTURE FOCUS: Review of Short Answers

Is Ann in class?	No, she isn't.
Are you ready?	Yes, I am.
Were they at the wedding party?	Yes, they were.
Was Tom angry?	No, he wasn't.
Do you have an English book?	Yes, I do.
Does this bus go to Main Street?	No, it doesn't.
Did Fran go running yesterday?	Yes, she did.
Have you read this book?	No, I haven't.
Has Fran been running for a year?	Yes, she has.
Can you play basketball?	No, I can't.
Will you help me?	Yes, I will.

1. Teacher models each question and answer, asking the student to listen to the short answer. Student listens.

2. Teacher models the question and answer. Student repeats the answer.

DRILL: Question and Answer Drill

Teacher asks a question which the student answers using a short answer. Student replies may be affirmative or negative.

Teacher	Student
Are the children playing ball?	
No, they aren't.	No, they aren't.
Have you read this book?	
Yes, I have.	Yes, I have.

Can you play baseball?
Will you help me?
Was Fran crying?
Can we be ready by nine o'clock?
Does Fran sometimes get tired from running?
Is Mike White still working?
Are Fran and Mike retired?
Did you take a driver's test for your license?
Will you drive me home, please?
Can Jason fix the stairs?
Has Fran been running for a year?
Will they paint the kitchen gray?
Has Steve saved some money?
Have you tried to telephone Ann today?

LISTENING COMPREHENSION

Fran White likes to run. She has been running every day for three years. She gets up at five o'clock and runs. Sometimes, she runs in the park. Sometimes, she runs in the street. She is getting ready for a big race. It is a mile race for retired women. Fran wants to win the race.

---

1. Teacher reads the story twice at a normal pace.
   Student listens. Student asks about words he does not know.

2. Student tells the story in his own words. If the student cannot tell the story, teacher may begin the sentence and have the student complete it.

Note: If the student cannot remember the story, read it once or twice again.

ORAL EVALUATION

1. Review measures of length by doing the Question and Answer Drill. Student should be able to answer 5 items.

2. Review terms for feelings by doing the Question and Answer Drill. Student should be able to answer all of the items.

3. Review the terms for running in a race. Ask questions that elicit the vocabulary items. Student should know 4 of them.

4. Review the vocabulary about the retired couple, asking questions that elicit the items. Student should know the meaning of retired.

5. Review signing and printing one's name. Student should be able to distinguish these terms and to recognize that both are writing.

6. Review the present perfect progressive tense by doing the drill on Answering Questions.

7. Review while clauses by doing the drill on Answering Questions.

II. Reading and Writing

SKILL BOOK 3: Lesson 12

Complete Lesson 12 in Skill Book 3, following the instructions given in the Laubach Way to Reading Teacher's Manual for Skill Book 3. Adapt the wording of the suggested teacher's instructions to the student as needed for your ESOL student's comprehension.

ADDITIONAL WRITTEN PRACTICE

After completing Lesson 12 in the skill book, have the student do the practices for Lesson 12 in the Workbook for Skill Book 3.

Lesson 13

OBJECTIVES

When a student completes this unit, he should be able to:

1. Say and respond to a new dialog.
2. Say some words related to church services.
3. Say some expressions of sympathy.
4. Say some words related to flying.
5. Say some words that name periods of time.
6. Use It + be + infinitive, as in It's time to eat.
7. Use It takes + time expressions + infinitive, as in It takes me an hour to get to work.
8. Make tag questions with be (is, are, was, were), as in It's a nice day, isn't it?
9. Give the expected answers to tag questions.
10. Make questions with why.
11. Listen to a story and repeat it in his own words.

VISUAL AIDS

1. ESOL Illustrations 3, pp. 36-39.
2. A watch, preferably with a second hand.
3. A calendar for a full year.

I. Conversation Skills

DIALOG

A: The weather is terrible.
   I hate rain.
B: Me, too.
   I haven't been able to go fishing all week.

A: You must like to fish.
B: Yes, it's my favorite way to spend my free time.

A: Where do you go fishing?
B: At Snake River.

A: That's a good place to fish, isn't it?
B: Yes, it is.

Mike and Fran go to church on Sunday.
They pray together.
They listen to the minister in church.
The minister leads the services in church.

When Fran's brother died, there was a funeral.
There were services in church for Fran's dead brother.
After the services, they went to the cemetery.
Friends put flowers on the grave.

Use ESOL Illustrations 3, pp. 36-37.

DRILL: Question and Answer Drill

Teacher asks questions to elicit vocabulary items.

Teacher	Student
Where do Mike and Fran go on Sunday? They go to church on Sunday.	They go to church on Sunday.
Who do Mike and Fran listen to in church? They listen to the minister.	They listen to the minister.

What does the minister do in church?
What was there in church when Fran's brother died?
Who do Mike and Fran listen to in church?
Who were the services in church for?
Where did they go after the services?
What did friends put on the grave?
What do people do in church?

VOCABULARY: Expressions of Sympathy

I lost all my money.	That's a shame.
She broke her leg.	What a pity.
The child was crying.	Her mother picked her up and said, "There, there."

---

1. Teacher models each pair of sentences. Student listens.

2. Teacher models each pair of sentences.
   Student repeats the expression of sympathy.

DRILL: Rejoinder Drill

Teacher makes a statement, to which the student replies with an expression of sympathy.

Teacher	Student
When a child is crying, what do you say? There, there.	There, there.
When Ed is sick, what do you say? What a pity.	What a pity.
When Kay loses her sweater, what do you say?	
When a child is crying, what do you say?	
When Steve loses his money, what do you say?	
When Ed is sick, what do you say?	

VOCABULARY: Flying

Mike and Fran are going to <u>fly</u> to King City.
They are going to fly on a big <u>airplane</u> high in the <u>sky</u>.
They will get their <u>tickets</u> at the <u>air line</u>.

Their <u>flight</u> to King City leaves at 9:30 <u>a.m.</u>
It is in the morning.

There is another flight to King City at 9:30 <u>p.m.</u>
It is at night.

The <u>pilot</u> will fly the plane.
The <u>flight</u> attendant will give them a cup of coffee.

Use <u>ESOL</u> Illustrations <u>3</u>, pp. 38-39.

DRILL: Question and Answer Drill

Teacher asks questions to elicit vocabulary items.

Teacher	Student
How are Mike and Fran going to King City? They are going to fly to King City.	They are going to fly to King City.
What are they going to fly on? They are going to fly on a big airplane.	They are going to fly on a big airplane.

Where will they get their tickets?
Who flies the plane?
Who gives Mike and Fran coffee?
When does their flight to King City leave?
How are Mike and Fran going to King City?
What are they going to fly on?

VOCABULARY: Time

There are 60 <u>seconds</u> in one <u>minute</u>.
There are 60 minutes in one <u>hour</u>.
There are 24 hours in one <u>day</u>.
There are 30 or 31 days in one <u>month</u>.
There are 12 months in one <u>year</u>.

Use a clock or watch and a calendar for a full year to explain the words.

DRILL: Answering Questions

Teacher asks questions which elicit the vocabulary being taught.

Teacher

How many seconds are there in a minute?
There are 60 seconds in a minute.

How many minutes are there in an hour?
There are 60 minutes in an hour.

How many hours are there in a day?
How many days are there in a month?
How many months are there in a year?
How many minutes are there in an hour?
How many seconds are there in a minute?

Student

There are 60 seconds in a minute.

There are 60 minutes in an hour.

STRUCTURE FOCUS: <u>It's</u> + <u>time</u> + (<u>for</u>) + <u>Infinitive</u>

It's time to eat.
It's time to go to bed.

It's time for Fran to run.
It's time for me to go to work.

As you model each sentence, ask the student to listen to <u>It's time to</u>.

DRILL: Making Sentences

Teacher has the student make sentences using <u>It's time</u> and <u>It's time to</u>.

Teacher

It's time
It's time to study.

It's time for Fran
It's time for Fran to run.

It's time for Mike
It's time for Mike and Fran
It's time for the teacher
It's time for you
It's time for my son (daughter)
It's time for me
It's time

Student

It's time to study.

It's time for Fran to run.

STRUCTURE FOCUS: <u>It</u> + <u>takes</u> + <u>Time Expressions</u> + <u>Infinitive</u>

<u>It</u> <u>takes</u> me	<u>30 minutes</u>	<u>to get</u> to work.	
<u>It</u> <u>takes</u> me	<u>an hour</u>	<u>to bake</u> a cake.	

As you model each sentence, ask the student to listen to <u>It takes</u>.

DRILL: <u>Answering Questions</u>

Teacher asks a question which the student answers using <u>It takes</u>.
Student replies may vary.

<u>Teacher</u>   <u>Student</u>

How long does it take you to get to work?
It takes me 30 minutes.   It takes me 30 minutes.

How long does it take you to bake a cake?
It takes me an hour.   It takes me an hour.

How long does it take you to get to work?
How long does it take you to get to class?
How long does it take you to get to the post office?
How long does it take you to get to your friend's house?
How long does it take you to make breakfast?
How long does it take you to make dinner?
How long does it take you to do dishes?
How long does it take you to do your homework?

STRUCTURE FOCUS: Tag Questions with be

It's a nice day, isn't it?
She was a waitress, wasn't she?
You are Italian, aren't you?
There are tomatoes in the salad, aren't there?

Carla wasn't going camping, was she?
You aren't married, are you?
Gail and Jason weren't here, were they?
We aren't leaving now, are we?

As you model each sentence, ask the student to listen to isn't it, wasn't she, and so on.

Note: When the first (statement) part of the sentence is affirmative,
the tag question is negative.

When the first part of the sentence is negative,
the tag question is affirmative.

Both verbs are in the same tense.
A pronoun is always used in the tag question.

DRILL: Making Questions

Teacher makes a statement to which the student adds a tag question.

Teacher	Student
It's a nice day. It's a nice day, isn't it?	It's a nice day, isn't it?
Ann wasn't sick. Ann wasn't sick, was she?	Ann wasn't sick, was she?

Carla wasn't going camping.
You are Italian.
Ray and Kay are married.
It wasn't a nice day yesterday.
We're leaving now.
Gail and Jason weren't here yesterday.
Ann wasn't sick.
There are tomatoes in the salad.
He's a minister.
There isn't any sugar in the tea.

STRUCTURE FOCUS: Expected Answers to Tag Questions

It's a nice day, isn't it?	Yes, it is.
You are married, aren't you?	Yes, I am.
Pete wasn't here yesterday, was he?	No, he wasn't.
Ann wasn't late, was she?	No, she wasn't.

1. Teacher models each question and answer,
   asking the student to listen to the answer.

2. Teacher models the question and answer. Student repeats each answer.

Note: Generally in tag questions, when confirmation or agreement is being
solicited, the short reply agrees with the statement. If it is an affirmative
statement, agreement is expressed with Yes. If it is a negative statement,
agreement is expressed with No.

Some students may not be accustomed to expressing agreement with No in similar
constructions in their own language and may think the answer should be Yes, he
wasn't.

DRILL: Answering Questions

Teacher asks a tag question, which the student answers using short answers.

Teacher   Student

It's a nice day, isn't it?
Yes, it is.   Yes, it is.

Pete wasn't here yesterday, was he?
No, he wasn't.   No, he wasn't.

Carla isn't going camping, is she?
You are Italian, aren't you?
Ray and Kay are married, aren't they?
It was a nice day yesterday, wasn't it?
There are tomatoes in the salad, aren't there?
We're leaving now, aren't we?
Gail and Jason weren't here yesterday, were they?
Ann wasn't sick, was she?
There isn't any sugar in the tea, is there?
He's a minister, isn't he?

STRUCTURE FOCUS: Questions with why

Fran runs five miles every day.
Why does Fran run five miles every day?

Lee hit the tree.
Why did Lee hit the tree?

Fran has been crying.
Why has Fran been crying?

---

1. Teacher models each pair of sentences, asking the student to listen to why.
2. Teacher models each pair of sentences. Student repeats the question with why.

DRILL: Making Questions

Teacher gives a statement which the student changes into a question with why.

Teacher

Fran has been crying.
Why has Fran been crying?

Steve saves some of his money.
Why does Steve save some of his money?

Fran runs five miles every day.
Mike White is at home.
Mrs. Green was angry at Lee.
Lee hit the tree.
Fran was crying.
They eat a lot of beans.
Jill has two part-time jobs.
You are studying English.

Student

Why has Fran been crying?

Why does Steve save some of his money?

LISTENING COMPREHENSION

   Tom Roberts died in his sleep one night. His family and
his friends were very sad to hear about Tom. They loved him,
and they missed him. They came to see Tom's wife Ellen to try
to help her. They talked about the good times they had with
Ellen and Tom. They cried together.
   Tom's family and friends went to the church services for
Tom. The minister said some nice things about Tom. It was a
sad day for everyone.

---

1. Teacher reads the story twice at a normal pace.
   Student listens. Student asks about words he does not know.

2. Student tells the story in his own words. If the student cannot tell the
   story, teacher may begin the sentence and have the student complete it.

Note: If the student cannot remember the story, read it once or twice again.

ORAL EVALUATION

1. Using <u>ESOL Illustrations 3</u>, pp. 36-37, review the vocabulary on church services by doing the Question and Answer Drill. Student should know 7 items.

2. Practice expressions of sympathy by doing the Rejoinder Drill. Student should know all of the items.

3. Using <u>ESOL Illustrations 3</u>, pp. 38-39, practice words about flying by doing the Question and Answer Drill. Student should know 8 of the items.

4. Review words about time by doing the drill on Answering Questions. Student should know all of the items.

5. Review <u>It's</u> + <u>time</u> + (<u>for</u>) + infinitive by doing the drill on Making Sentences.

6. Review <u>It</u> + <u>takes</u> + time expressions + infinitive by doing the drill on Answering Questions.

7. Review the use of tag questions with <u>be</u> by doing the drill on Making Questions.

8. Review the expected answers to tag questions by doing the drill on Answering Questions.

9. Review questions with <u>why</u> by doing the drill on Making Questions.

<u>II. Reading and Writing</u>

<u>SKILL BOOK 3</u>: Lesson 13

Complete Lesson 13 in <u>Skill Book 3</u>, following the instructions given in the Laubach Way to Reading <u>Teacher's Manual for Skill Book 3</u>. Adapt the wording of the suggested teacher's instructions to the student as needed for your ESOL student's comprehension.

<u>ADDITIONAL WRITTEN PRACTICE</u>

After completing Lesson 13 in the skill book, have the student do the practices for Lesson 13 in the <u>Workbook for Skill Book 3</u>.

Lesson 14

OBJECTIVES

When a student completes this unit, he should be able to:

1. Say and respond to a new dialog.
2. Use get and some adjectives.
3. Use words having to do with an air line timetable.
4. Use the phrase in sight.
5. Use some adjectives: worry, afraid, angry, interested, tired, right, wrong.
6. Use adjectives + prepositions + nouns, as in She is angry at Lee.
7. Use should in affirmative and negative statements, questions, and short answers.
8. Use tag questions with do, does, did.
9. Use tag questions with other verbs.
10. Use because in answers to questions with why.
11. Use as...as with adjectives and adverbs, as in Fran runs as fast as Kim does.
12. Listen to a story and repeat it in his own words.

VISUAL AIDS

The air line timetable in Skill Book 3, p. 75.

I. Conversation Skills

DIALOG
_____

A: Excuse me.
   Can you tell me where the plane to Dallas is?
B: It departs from Gate 5.

A: Pardon me.
B: The plane for Dallas leaves from Gate 5.

A: Where is Gate 5?
B: Turn left, and walk past Gates 1, 2, and 3.

A: Thank you.
B: You're welcome.
_____

VOCABULARY: <u>get</u> + <u>Adjectives</u>

It	<u>is getting</u>	<u>cold</u>.	
My son	<u>is getting</u>	<u>tall</u>.	
They	<u>got</u>	<u>ready</u>	to paint.
My hair	<u>is getting</u>	<u>gray</u>.	

<u>Note</u>: The verb <u>get</u>, followed by certain adjectives, means <u>become</u>.

<u>DRILL</u>: <u>Making Sentences</u>

Teacher names an adjective, and the student uses it in a sentence with <u>get</u>.

<u>Teacher</u>	<u>Student</u>
old	
I am getting old.	I am getting old.
gray	
My hair is getting gray.	My hair is getting gray.
cold	
light	
well	
dark	
fast	

VOCABULARY: <u>Air Line Timetable</u>

Air lines have a <u>timetable</u> of flights to and from many cities.
The <u>timetable</u> tells when the air line <u>departs</u> and when it <u>arrives</u>.
The <u>timetable</u> tells which <u>gate</u> the airplane will be at.

Use <u>Skill</u> <u>Book</u> <u>3</u>, p. 75, to show an air line timetable.

VOCABULARY: <u>The Use of</u> <u>in sight</u>

I can see the church from here.
It's <u>in sight</u>.

Lee can see the lights of his city from the airplane.
They are still <u>in sight</u>.

The river is very far from here.
It's not <u>in sight</u>.

VOCABULARY: Adjectives about Feelings

Pete is <u>worried</u>. His mother is very sick.
Mrs. Green is <u>angry</u>. It's half past three, and Lee isn't home.
Ed was <u>afraid</u>. Lee was driving the car very fast.
Carla was <u>right</u>. She said I needed a license to drive a car.
Ed was <u>wrong</u>. He said I didn't need a license to drive a car.
I am <u>tired</u>. I worked ten hours today.
I am <u>interested</u>. This book is very good.

STRUCTURE FOCUS: Adjectives + Prepositions + Nouns

Pete is	worried about	his mother.
Mrs. Green is	angry at	Lee.
Ed is	afraid of	the dog.
Carla was	right about	the time.
Ed was	wrong about	the price.
I am	tired of	television.
I am	interested in	good books.

As you model each sentence, ask the student to listen to <u>worry about</u>, <u>angry at</u>, and so on.

DRILL: Answering Questions

Teacher asks questions which elicit an adjective + preposition in the answer.

Teacher	Student
What is Pete worried about? He's worried about his mother.	He's worried about his mother.
Who is Mrs. Green angry at? She's angry at Lee.	She's angry at Lee.
What is Ed afraid of? What was Carla right about? What was Ed wrong about? What is Pete worried about? Who is Mrs. Green angry at? What are you tired of? What are you interested in?	

STRUCTURE FOCUS: Adjectives + Prepositions + Verb-ing

Lee Chan is	worried about	leaving his country.
Ed is	afraid of	swimming in cold water.
I am	tired of	watching TV.
I am	interested in	learning about China.

As you model each sentence, ask the student to listen to the -ing: leaving, swimming, watching, and learning.

DRILL: Making Questions

Teacher asks questions which elicit adjectives + prepositions + verb-ing.

Teacher	Student
What is Lee Chan worried about? He's worried about leaving China.	He's worried about leaving China.
What is Ed afraid of? He's afraid of swimming in cold water.	He's afraid of swimming in cold water.
What is Lee Chan worried about? What is Ed afraid of? What is Fran interested in? What are you tired of? What are you interested in?	

STRUCTURE FOCUS: The Use of should

You should stop smoking.
They should listen to their parents.

You shouldn't smoke.
Ann shouldn't spend a lot of money.

Should I buy the red dress? No, you shouldn't.
Should we leave now?   Yes, we should.

As you model each statement or question-and-answer, ask the student to listen to should--or shouldn't. Explain what smoking means.

Note: Should is used to express advisability; however, we do not very often do the things we say we should.

DRILL: Making Questions

Teacher gives a statement, which the student must change into the question form and then answer.

Teacher

You should stop smoking.
    Should I stop smoking?
    Yes, I should.

Ann should buy the red dress.
    Should Ann buy the red dress?
    No, she shouldn't.

We should leave now.
We should pay our bills.
Lee should pay for the tree.
Pete should fix the radio.
Ann should leave early.
Carla should study her lesson.
Ed should get a driver's license.
Mike should make breakfast.
Ann should spend a lot of money.

Student

Should I stop smoking?
Yes, I should.

Should Ann buy the red dress?
No, she shouldn't.

STRUCTURE FOCUS: Tag Questions with <u>do</u>, <u>does</u>, <u>did</u>

The Masons have to pay a lot of bills, <u>don't they</u>?
You don't have to have license plates for a bicycle, <u>do you</u>?
Gail and Jason rented an apartment, <u>didn't they</u>?
Lee didn't see the tree, <u>did he</u>?

As you model each sentence, ask the student to listen to the tag question.

DRILL: Making Questions

Teacher gives a statement, to which the student adds a tag question.

Teacher	Student

Lee has to pay for the tree.
   Lee has to pay for the tree,
   doesn't he?
	Lee has to pay for the tree,
	doesn't he?

Lee didn't see the tree.
   Lee didn't see the tree,
   did he?
	Lee didn't see the tree,
	did he?

Fran cried about her brother.
Tom Roberts died in his sleep.
The Masons have to pay a lot of bills.
Ann goes to class at night.
You live near the school.
You have to take tests to get a driver's license.

STRUCTURE FOCUS: Tag Questions with Other Verbs

Jason and Gail have never painted a kitchen, have they?
Fran has been running a long time, hasn't she?

You can fix the radio, can't you?
Lee can't play hockey, can he?

They will play hockey in Canada, won't they?
Lee will not be late again, will he?

Ann should stop smoking, shouldn't she?
Tom shouldn't spend so much money, should he?

As you model each sentence, ask the student to listen to the tag question.

DRILL: Making Questions

Teacher gives a statement, to which the student adds a tag question.

Teacher	Student

You can fix the radio.
    You can fix the radio,
    can't you?
	You can fix the radio,
	can't you?

Fran hasn't been playing soccer.
    Fran hasn't been playing soccer,
    has she?
	Fran hasn't been playing soccer,
	has she?

Tom shouldn't spend so much money.
Lee will not be late again.
Gail and Jason have never painted a kitchen.
You can fix the radio.
Ann should stop smoking.
Retired people can get things for cheaper prices.
They will play hockey in Canada.
Fran has been running a long time.

STRUCTURE FOCUS: Because Clauses

Why is Lee Chan sad?
Because he is leaving his family.

Why was Fran crying?
Because her brother died in his sleep.

Why does Fran run five miles every day?
Because she wants to win the race.

---

1. Teacher models each question and answer, asking the student to listen to because. Student listens.

2. Teacher models each question and answer. Student repeats the answer.

DRILL: Question and Answer Drill

Teacher asks a question, which the student answers using because.
Student replies may vary.

Teacher	Student
Why is Lee Chan sad?	
Because he is leaving his family.	Because he is leaving his family.
Why does Gail have two part-time jobs?	
Because she needs the money.	Because she needs the money.

Why was Fran crying?
Why does Fran run five miles every day?
Why does Mike White stay at home?
Why was Mrs. Green angry at Lee?
Why did Lee hit the tree?
Why are you studying English?

STRUCTURE FOCUS: <u>as</u> + <u>Adjective/Adverb</u> + <u>as</u>

This pencil is	<u>as</u> long <u>as</u>	that one.
This book is	<u>as</u> big <u>as</u>	that one.
Her hair is	<u>as</u> dark <u>as</u>	Gail's.
Mrs. Green is	<u>as</u> angry <u>as</u>	I am.
Fran runs	<u>as</u> fast <u>as</u>	Kim does.

As you model each sentence, ask the student to listen to <u>as</u>...<u>as</u>.

Note: <u>As</u>...<u>as</u> is used with adjectives and adverbs to discuss two people or things that are alike. Show the students two objects that are the same length or size, such as two pencils or books.

DRILL: Combining Sentences

Teacher gives two sentences, which the student combines using <u>as</u>...<u>as</u>.

Teacher   Student

Pete is sad.
Lee is sad.
Pete is as sad as Lee.   Pete is as sad as Lee.

This book is big.
That book is big.
This book is as big as that one.   This book is as big as that one.

Jane's hair is dark.
Gail's hair is dark.

Mrs. Green is angry.
I am angry.

Fran is happy.
Mike is happy.

Fran runs fast.
Kim runs fast.

Chan speaks slowly.
I speak slowly.

Pete is sad.
Lee is sad.

This book is small.
That book is small.

LISTENING COMPREHENSION

Lee Chan is from China. He left China to study in the United States. He left his wife and child in China. He will not see them for four years. It makes Lee sad to think of his family.

Lee is going to study hard. He wants to have a better job when he goes back to China. He wants to take care of his family better. And he wants to help China.

---

1. Teacher reads the story twice at a normal pace.
   Student listens. Student asks about words he does not know.

2. Student tells the story in his own words. If the student cannot tell the story, teacher may begin the sentence and have the student complete it.

Note: If the student cannot remember the story, read it once or twice again.

ORAL EVALUATION

1. Review the use of get + adjectives. Student should know all items.
2. Using the timetable in Skill Book 3, p. 54, have the student identify words about timetables. Student should know all items.
3. Review the adjectives. Student should know all of them.
4. Review adjectives + prepositions + nouns by doing the drill on Making Questions.
5. Review adjectives + prepositions + verb-ing by doing the drill on Making Questions.
6. Review should by doing the drill on Making Questions.
7. Review tag questions with do, does, and did by doing the drill on Making Questions.
8. Review tag questions with other verbs by doing the drill on Making Questions.
9. Review because clauses by doing the Question and Answer Drill.
10. Review as + adjective/adverb + as by doing the drill on Combining Sentences.

II. Reading and Writing

SKILL BOOK 3: Lesson 14

Complete Lesson 14 in Skill Book 3, following the instructions given in the Laubach Way to Reading Teacher's Manual for Skill Book 3. Adapt the wording of the suggested teacher's instructions to the student as needed for your ESOL student's comprehension.

ADDITIONAL WRITTEN PRACTICE

After completing Lesson 14 in the skill book, have the student do the practices for Lesson 14 in the Workbook for Skill Book 3.

Lesson 15

<u>OBJECTIVES</u>

When a student completes this unit, he should be able to:

1. Say and respond to a new dialog.
2. Use the word <u>almost.</u>
3. Use words about driving a car.
4. Use irregular noun plurals: <u>knives</u>, <u>wives</u>, <u>leaves</u>, <u>loaves</u>, <u>shelves</u>, and <u>men</u>, <u>women</u>, <u>children</u>, <u>feet</u>, <u>teeth</u>.
5. Use the comparative of adjectives.
6. Use the comparative of <u>good</u>, <u>bad</u>, <u>little</u>, and <u>far</u>.
7. Use <u>something/anything</u> + adjective + infinitive, as in <u>I</u> <u>want</u> <u>something</u> <u>hot</u> <u>to</u> <u>drink</u>.
8. Use <u>think</u> and <u>say</u> + noun clauses, as in <u>I</u> <u>think</u> <u>that</u> <u>he</u> <u>is</u> <u>a</u> <u>fine</u> <u>person</u>.
9. Listen to a story and repeat it in his own words.

<u>VISUAL AIDS</u>

1. An I.D. card or a driver's license or both.
2. Two small markers that can be used to represent cars, or two toy cars.

<u>I. Conversation Skills</u>

<u>DIALOG</u>

A: Would you cash this check for me, please?
B: Do you have an account at this bank?

A: Yes, I have a savings account.
B: Do you have any I.D.?

A: What?
B: Do you have any identification?

A: I have a driver's license.
    And I have an I.D. card from work.
    It has my picture on it.
B: Oh, good. Those are fine.

VOCABULARY: <u>The Use of almost</u>

It's 8:45. It's <u>almost</u> 9 o'clock.
My birthday is next month. I'm going to be 35. I'm <u>almost</u> 35.
I will be ready in five minutes. I'm <u>almost</u> ready.

---

1. Teacher models each group of 2-3 sentences, asking the student to listen to <u>almost</u>. Student listens.

2. Teacher models each group of sentences. Student repeats each sentence.

DRILL: <u>Expansion Drill</u>

Teacher makes a statement, to which the student adds the word <u>almost</u>.

<u>Teacher</u>	<u>Student</u>
I am 35.	
I am almost 35.	I am almost 35.
It is 9 o'clock.	
It is almost 9 o'clock.	It is almost 9 o'clock.

It's 10 o'clock.
I am 35.
I am ready.
He is finished.
It's October.
It's time to stop work.

VOCABULARY: <u>Driving a Car</u>

Jill is learning how to drive a car.
She is learning how to go <u>forward</u>.
She is learning how to <u>back up</u>.
She is learning to make <u>left</u> and <u>right</u> <u>turns</u>.
She is learning to <u>pass</u> other cars.
She is learning to <u>park</u> the car.

Demonstrate the meaning of the new words, using small markers to represent cars or toy cars.

STRUCTURE FOCUS: Irregular Noun Plurals

knife	knives	I have a knife.
		I have two knives.
wife	wives	I have a wife.
		My two sons have wives.
leaf	leaves	I have a leaf.
		I have two leaves.
loaf	loaves	I have a loaf of bread.
		I have two loaves of bread.
shelf	shelves	I have a shelf.
		I have two shelves.

1. Teacher models each pair of words.
   Explain the meaning of any words the student does not know.

2. Teacher models each pair of sentences.
   Student repeats after each sentence.

DRILL: Transformation Drill

Teacher gives a sentence in the singular, which the student changes into the plural, using the number two.

Teacher	Student
I have a knife.	
I have two knives.	I have two knives.
There is a wife.	
There are two wives.	There are two wives.
There is a leaf on the tree.	
There is a loaf of bread in the kitchen.	
There is a shelf in the room.	
There is a wife.	
I have a knife.	

STRUCTURE FOCUS: More Irregular Noun Plurals

---

child	children	I have a child.
		I have two children.
man	men	A man is in the room.
		Two men are in the room.
woman	women	A woman is behind the table.
		Two women are behind the table.
foot	feet	My foot hurts.
		My feet hurt.
tooth	teeth	My tooth aches.
		My teeth ache.

---

1. Teacher models each pair of words.
   Explain the meaning of any words the student does not know.

2. Teacher models each pair of sentences.
   Student repeats after each sentence.

DRILL: Transformation Drill

Teacher gives a sentence in the singular which the student changes into the plural.

Teacher	Student
The child is happy.	
The children are happy.	The children are happy.
My foot hurts.	
My feet hurt.	My feet hurt.
My tooth aches.	
The man is in the room.	
The woman is behind the table.	
The child is happy.	
My foot hurts.	

STRUCTURE FOCUS: something/anything + Adjective + Infinitive

Ellen has	something	sad	to tell you.
I want	something	hot	to drink.
I don't have	anything	clean	to wear.
I can't find	anything	interesting	to read.

As you model each sentence, ask the student to listen to something sad to tell you, and so on.

DRILL: Making Questions

Teacher gives the beginning of a question, such as Do you have something nice. Student completes the question with an infinitive or infinitive phrase.

Teacher

Do you want something hot
Do you want something hot to drink?

Do you have something good
Do you have something good to tell me?

Do you have something nice
Does Ellen have something sad
Do you have something green
Do you want something cold
Do you have something green
Can you find anything clean
Can you find anything interesting

Student

Do you want something hot to drink?

Do you have something good to tell me?

STRUCTURE FOCUS: think or say + Noun Clauses

I think that he is a fine person.
Lee thinks that prices are high in the United States.
Ellen said that Tom died in his sleep.
They said that Tom was a fine man.

As you model each sentence, ask the student to listen to think that or said that.

Note: These noun clauses are objects of the verb think or say. The word that has no meaning in itself and is often omitted.

DRILL: Making Sentences

Teacher makes a statement and gives a subject. The student must make a statement with think or say and a noun clause.

Teacher	Student
Mike is a fine man. (I) I think that Mike is a fine man.	I think that Mike is a fine man.
Tom died in his sleep. (Ellen) Ellen said that Tom died in his sleep.	Ellen said that Tom died in his sleep.
Prices in the United States are high. (Lee)	
Jill did not stop at a stop sign. (The tester)	
I am ready for the mile race. (I)	
It was OK for Fran to run. (The doctor)	
Mike is a fine man. (You)	
Tom died in his sleep. (Ellen)	

LISTENING COMPREHENSION

Ellen and Tom Roberts had a happy life together. They
were married for 29 years. And then Tom died in his sleep one
night. Ellen was very sad, and she cried and cried. Her family
helped her at first. But then they had to leave, and she was
alone. Ellen had to learn to live by herself. She had to find a
job. She had to start a new life for herself.

---

1. Teacher reads the story twice at a normal pace.
   Student listens. Student asks about words he does not know.

2. Student tells the story in his own words. If the student cannot tell the
   story, teacher may begin the sentence and have the student complete it.

Note: If the student cannot remember the story, read it once or twice again.

ORAL EVALUATION

1. Review the use of almost by doing the Expansion Drill.
2. By demonstrating the verbs, review the vocabulary on driving a car.
   Student should know 4 of the items.
3. Review the irregular noun plurals by doing both Transformation Drills.
   Student should know 8 of the items.
4. Review the comparative of good, bad, little, and far, by doing the drill on
   Combining Sentences.
5. Review something/anything + adjective + infinitive by doing the drill on
   Making Questions.
6. Review think and say + noun clauses by doing the drill on Making Sentences.

II. Reading and Writing

SKILL BOOK 3: Lesson 15

Complete Lesson 15 in Skill Book 3, following the instructions given in the
Laubach Way to Reading Teacher's Manual for Skill Book 3. Adapt the wording of
the suggested teacher's instructions to the student as needed for your ESOL
student's comprehension.

ADDITIONAL WRITTEN PRACTICE

After completing Lesson 15 in the skill book, have the student do the practices
for Lesson 15 in the Workbook for Skill Book 3.

Lesson 16

<u>OBJECTIVES</u>

When a student completes this unit, he should be able to:

1. Say and respond to a new dialog.
2. Say the story words <u>gold</u> and <u>silver</u>.
3. Use the expressions <u>Oh</u>; <u>Oh</u>, <u>no</u>; and <u>Oh</u>, <u>well</u>.
4. Say the names of some city workers.
5. Use the word <u>both</u>.
6. Say the past participle of irregular verbs: <u>break</u> (<u>broken</u>), <u>choose</u> (<u>chosen</u>), <u>drive</u> (<u>driven</u>), <u>freeze</u> (<u>frozen</u>), <u>ride</u> (<u>ridden</u>), and <u>steal</u> (<u>stolen</u>).
7. Use the passive voice.
8. Use the passive with <u>get</u>, as in <u>I got tired</u>.
9. Use <u>can</u> and <u>could</u>.
10. Use <u>if</u> clauses, as in <u>I can't tell if he is right</u>.
11. Use clauses with <u>so</u>, as in <u>I am tired, so I am going to bed</u>.
12. Listen to a story and repeat it in his own words.

<u>VISUAL AIDS</u>

1. <u>ESOL Illustrations 3</u>, pp. 40-41.
2. A gold ring.
3. A silver ring.

<u>I. Conversation Skills</u>

<u>DIALOG</u>

A: I need a new sofa, but I don't have much money.
B: Why don't you look at the ads in the paper?

A: What's in the ads?
B: Sometimes they have sofas that people want to sell.
   They cost less than new ones.

A: That's what I need--a sofa that costs less.
   I don't have the money for a new sofa.
B: I bet you'll find a cheap one in the ads.

A: Thanks for the advice.

<u>VOCABULARY</u>: Gold and Silver

<u>Gold</u> rings are expensive.
Usually, <u>silver</u> rings cost less than gold rings.

Use a gold ring and a silver ring to show the meaning of the new words.

VOCABULARY: Expressions with <u>Oh</u>

Oh, <u>good</u>! I have a letter from my sister.
<u>Oh</u>, <u>my head</u>! It really hurts.
<u>Oh</u>, <u>no</u>! I have a parking ticket.
Joe isn't home. <u>Oh</u>, <u>well</u>. I'll call him later.
Fran didn't win the race. <u>Oh</u>, <u>well</u>, she can try again.

Act out the meaning of the expressions. Say the words with feeling.

DRILL: Rejoinder Drill

Teacher makes a statement which elicits an expression with <u>Oh</u> from the student.

Teacher	Student
I have a letter from my sister. Oh, good.	Oh, good.
Our team lost the game. Oh, no.	Oh, no.
I didn't see Joe. Oh, well. You can try again tomorrow.	Oh, well. You can try again tomorrow.
I hurt my leg. I have a parking ticket. I don't have any money. Fran didn't win the race. Joe isn't home. My baby is feeling better. My TV isn't working.	

VOCABULARY: Public Employees

<u>Police officers</u> work for the police department.
They carry guns.

<u>Firefighters</u> work for the fire department.
They put water on burning buildings.

<u>Sanitation workers</u> clean the city streets.

<u>Mail carriers</u> bring letters to our homes.

Use <u>ESOL Illustrations 3</u>, pp. 40-41.

DRILL: Identification Drill

Using <u>ESOL Illustrations 3</u>, pp. 40-41, teacher asks, "Who are they?" and "What do they do?" Student replies may vary.

VOCABULARY: The Use of both

```
          Two police officers arrived quickly.
          Both of them had guns.

          Two books were on the table.
          Both of them were open.

          Ann and I are going to the movies.
          Both of us like to go to the movies.
```

Use p. 40 of ESOL Illustrations 3 for the police officers, and use actual books. Explain that both refers to two.

DRILL: Rejoinder Drill

Teacher makes a statement, to which the student replies using both.

Teacher	Student
Gail and Jason painted the chairs. Both of them like to paint.	Both of them like to paint.
Two police officers arrived quickly. Both of them had guns.	Both of them had guns.

Ann and Kim are going to the movies.
Ray and Kay go camping.
Pete and Steve work in the repair shop.
Gail and Jason painted the chairs.
Two police officers arrived quickly.
Fran and Mike were sad that Tom died.
Carla and David went to a dinner party for Carla's class.
You and Ann are good students.

VOCABULARY: Past Participles of Irregular Verbs

```
          break     broke     broken
          choose    chose     chosen
          drive     drove     driven
          freeze    froze     frozen
          ride      rode      ridden
          steal     stole     stolen
```

1. Teacher models all three forms of each verb in a sentence as student listens. Explain the meaning of any verbs the student does not understand.

2. Teacher models all three forms of each verb. Student repeats.

VOCABULARY: Past Participles of Irregular Verbs

Ed broke a glass yesterday.
He has broken many glasses.

Gail chose pink paint.
Gail has chosen many paints.

Pete drove the car very fast.
Pete has driven that car for a long time.

We froze the meat.
We have frozen the meat.

They rode to the bank on the bus.
They have ridden to school with Jason every week.

Someone stole Tony's ring last week.
Someone has stolen my coat.

---

1. Teacher models the sentences in pairs. Student listens.
2. Teacher models the sentences. Student repeats after each sentence.

DRILL: Answering Questions

Teacher asks a question in the present perfect tense, which the student answers
in the negative.

Teacher	Student
Have you broken anything today? No, I haven't broken anything today.	No, I haven't broken anything today.
Have you chosen a book to read? No, I haven't chosen one.	No, I haven't chosen one.

Have you ever driven a truck?
Have you frozen the meat?
Have you ever ridden in a truck?
Have you ever stolen anything?
Have you ever broken something in a store?
Have you chosen a book to read?

<u>STRUCTURE FOCUS</u>: The Passive Voice

<u>Active</u>	<u>Passive</u>
Someone steals the ring.	The ring is stolen.
Someone broke the lock.	The lock was broken.

1. Teacher models each pair of sentences, first the active and then the passive.

2. Teacher models each pair of sentences.
   Student repeats the passive sentence.

<u>Note</u>: The passive voice is formed by using the verb <u>be</u> and the past participle of the main verb. In the passive, the object of the active verb becomes the subject of the passive verb.

<u>DRILL</u>: <u>Transformation Drill</u>

Teacher gives an active sentence, which the student must change to the passive.

<u>Teacher</u>	<u>Student</u>
Someone stole the book. The book was stolen.	The book was stolen.
People speak English in many countries. English is spoken in many countries.	English is spoken in many countries.
Someone wrote this book. Someone drove the truck. Someone broke the lock. Someone stole the book. People speak English in many countries.	

STRUCTURE FOCUS: Passive Voice with get

She	got	tired.
They	are getting	married.
Mrs. Green	got	upset.
They	get	paid at the end of the month.
Nobody	got	hurt.
She	gets	worried when Lee is late.

As you model each sentence, ask the student to listen to get.

DRILL: Making Sentences

Teacher gives words which the student must use in a sentence.

Teacher	Student
get upset	
I get upset when I am tired.	I get upset when I am tired.
get tired	
Ann got tired.	Ann got tired.

get tired
get paid
get hurt
get worried
get upset

STRUCTURE FOCUS: The Use of can and could

I can speak Italian now.
I could speak Italian when I was a child.

He can play hockey now.
He could play hockey when he was young.

1. Teacher models each pair of sentences, asking the student to listen to can and could. Student listens.

2. Teacher models the sentences. Student repeats after each sentence.

<u>STRUCTURE FOCUS</u>: The Use of <u>could</u> and <u>couldn't</u>

<u>Could</u> you speak English when you were a child?
<u>No, I couldn't</u>.

<u>Could</u> Lee Chan read Chinese when he was young?
Yes, he <u>could</u>.

---

1. Teacher models each question and answer, asking the student to listen to <u>could</u> and <u>couldn't</u>.

2. Teacher models the sentences. Student repeats after each sentence.

<u>DRILL</u>: Transformation Drill

Teacher gives statement, which the student must change to the question form and then answer.

Teacher	Student
Fran could not run five miles at first. Could Fran run five miles at first? No, she couldn't.	Could Fran run five miles at first? No, she couldn't.
Gail and Jason could paint the kitchen. Could Gail and Jason paint the kitchen? Yes, they could.	Could Gail and Jason paint the kitchen? Yes, they could.

Pete could play hockey when he was young.
Steve could fix radios before he worked for Pete.
Lee Green could pay for the tree.
The police couldn't find Tony's clock radio.
I could speak Spanish when I was young.
I could speak English when I was a child.
Lee Chan could read Chinese when he was a child.

STRUCTURE FOCUS: If Clauses

```
I can't tell    if he is right.
I can't tell    if anyone is in the room.
We'll see       if anyone can help us.
I'll ask Carla  if she can cook for us.
```

As you model each sentence, ask the student to listen to if.

DRILL: Answering Questions

Teacher asks questions, which the student must answer using the words given to begin the sentence.

Teacher   Student

Is he right? I can't tell.
I can't tell if he is right.   I can't tell if he is right.

Can anyone help us? We'll see.
We'll see if anyone can help us.   We'll see if anyone can help us.

Is anyone at home? I can't tell.
Can Carla cook for us? I'll ask Carla.
Does Ed want to watch TV? I'll see.
Is she crying? I can't tell.
Is it raining outside? I can't tell.
Is he right? I can't tell.
Can Jason help us with our homework? I'll ask Jason.
Can anyone help us? We'll see.

STRUCTURE FOCUS: Clauses with <u>so</u>

I am tired, <u>so</u> I am going to bed.
Ellen's husband died, <u>so</u> she is very sad.
It was his mother's ring, <u>so</u> he loved it.

As you model each sentence, ask the student to listen to <u>so</u>.

DRILL: Combining Sentences

Teacher gives two sentences, which the student must combine using <u>so</u>.

<u>Teacher</u>   <u>Student</u>

I am tired.
I am going to bed.
I am tired, so I am going to bed.   I am tired, so I am going to bed.

My TV is broken.
I can't watch it.
My TV is broken, so I can't watch it.   My TV is broken, so I can't watch it.

It was his mother's ring.
He loved it.

Lee wants to learn English.
He is studying hard.

Ellen's husband died.
She is very sad.

My radio is broken.
Steve is going to fix it.

I'm not hungry.
I'm not going to have dinner.

I am tired.
I am going to bed.

My TV is broken.
I can't watch it.

LISTENING COMPREHENSION

Tony Romano lived in a big apartment building. One evening, Tony got back to his apartment very late. The door was open, and the lock was broken. He called the police.

Tony looked at his apartment. His sofa was stolen. His color TV and clock radio were stolen. A gold ring was missing.

Tony was sad because so many things were stolen.

---

1. Teacher reads the story twice at a normal pace.
   Student listens. Student asks about words he does not know.

2. Student tells the story in his own words. If the student cannot tell the story, teacher may begin the sentence and have the student complete it.

Note: If the student cannot remember the story, read it once or twice again.

ORAL EVALUATION

1. Review the expressions with Oh by doing the Rejoinder Drill.
2. Using ESOL Illustrations 3, pp. 40-41, review the names of public employees. Student should know all of them.
3. Review the use of both by doing the Rejoinder Drill.
4. Review the past participles of irregular verbs by doing the drill on Answering Questions.
5. Review the passive voice by doing the Transformation Drill.
6. Review the passive with get by doing the drill on Making Questions.
7. Review if clauses by doing the drill on Answering Questions.
8. Review the use of could by doing the Transformation Drill.
9. Review clauses with so by doing the drill on Combining Sentences.

II. Reading and Writing

SKILL BOOK 3: Lesson 16

Complete Lesson 16 in Skill Book 3, following the instructions given in the Laubach Way to Reading Teacher's Manual for Skill Book 3. Adapt the wording of the suggested teacher's instructions to the student as needed for your ESOL student's comprehension.

ADDITIONAL WRITTEN PRACTICE

After completing Lesson 16 in the skill book, have the student do the practices for Lesson 16 in the Workbook for Skill Book 3.

Lesson 17

OBJECTIVES

When a student completes this unit, he should be able to:

1. Say and respond to a new dialog.
2. Say some words about sleepwear.
3. Say some words about bedding.
4. Say the past participle of these irregular verbs: shake (shaken), speak (spoken), take (taken), wake (waked), write (wrote).
5. Use hope + that clause, as in I hope that it won't rain today.
6. Use adjective + that clause.
7. Use so as a substitute in the expressions I hope so and I think so.
8. Listen to a story and repeat it in his own words.

VISUAL AIDS

Use ESOL Illustrations 3, pp. 42-43.

I. Conversation Skills

DIALOG

```
A: This is Rose Jones.
   There's a fire in my home.
   It's at 1428 Valley Drive.
   The fire is in the kitchen.

B: Where are you?
A: I'm phoning from next door.

B: Is anyone in your house?
A: No, but I can't find my dog.

B: Don't worry about the dog.
   Don't go back home.
   Don't try to save anything.
A: Please hurry.
```

VOCABULARY: Sleepwear

Joe wears <u>pajamas</u> to bed.
Rose wears a <u>nightgown</u> to bed.
Joe wears a <u>robe</u> and <u>slippers</u> in the morning.
Rose wears a <u>robe</u> and <u>slippers</u> in the morning.

Use p. 42 of <u>ESOL Illustrations 3</u> for the new vocabulary.

DRILL: Identification Drill

Using p. 42 of <u>ESOL Illustrations 3</u>, ask the student "What's this?" to elicit vocabulary items.

VOCABULARY: Bedding

My bed has a hard <u>mattress</u>.
I put <u>sheets</u> on the mattress.
I put a <u>blanket</u> over the sheets.
I sleep with my head on a <u>pillow</u>.

Use p. 43 of <u>ESOL Illustrations 3</u> for the new vocabulary.

DRILL: Identification Drill

Using p. 43 of <u>ESOL Illustrations 3</u>, ask "What's this?" to elicit the vocabulary items.

<u>VOCABULARY</u>: <u>Past Participles of Irregular Verbs</u>

shake	shook	shaken
speak	spoke	spoken
take	took	taken
wake	woke	waked
write	wrote	written

1. Teacher models all three forms of each verb.
   Explain any verbs the student does not understand. Student listens.

2. Teacher models all three forms of each verb. Student repeats.

<u>Note</u>: For the past participle of <u>wake</u>, the form <u>woken</u> is also acceptable. If this is the form you always use, substitute it here and in the following drill.

<u>DRILL</u>: <u>Answering Questions</u>

Teacher asks a question in the present perfect tense, which the student answers in the negative.

<u>Teacher</u>

Have you ever spoken to Ellen?
   No, I have never spoken to Ellen.

Have you ever shaken hands with Mr. Chan?
   No, I have never shaken hands
   with Mr. Chan.

Have you ever taken a Chinese class?
Have you ever waked up before the sun?
Have you ever written a letter in English?
Have you ever shaken hands with Mr. Chan?
Have you ever spoken to Ellen?

<u>Student</u>

No, I have never spoken to Ellen.

No, I have never shaken hands
with Mr. Chan.

STRUCTURE FOCUS: <u>hope</u> + <u>that</u> Clause

I <u>hope</u> that they can save Rose and Joe's house.
I <u>hope</u> that I can go camping for three days.
I <u>hope</u> that it won't rain today.

As you model each sentence, ask the student to listen to <u>hope</u>.

DRILL: <u>Making Sentences</u>

Teacher gives words which student must use in a sentence with <u>I hope that</u>.

Teacher	Student
It won't rain today.	
I hope that it won't rain today.	I hope that it won't rain today.
I will see you again.	
I hope that I will see you again.	I hope that I will see you again.

I have learned my lesson.
I can go camping for three days.
I can get a new winter coat.
The firefighters can save Rose and Joe's house.
Ellen won't be sad.
Fran will win the race.
It won't rain today.
I will see you again.

STRUCTURE FOCUS: <u>so</u> <u>as</u> <u>a</u> <u>Substitute</u>

Do you think it will be sunny today?   I hope so.
                                            I think so.

Do you think they will save Rose and Joe's house?   I hope so.
                                            I think so.

Do you hope that Fran will win the race?   I hope so.
                                            I think so.

---

1. Teacher models each question and both of its answers, asking the student to listen to <u>I</u> <u>hope</u> <u>so</u> and <u>I</u> <u>think</u> <u>so</u>. Student listens.

2. Teacher models the question and its answers. Student repeats each answer.

DRILL: <u>Question</u> <u>and</u> <u>Answer</u> <u>Drill</u>

Teacher asks a question which the student answers using <u>I</u> <u>hope</u> <u>so</u> or <u>I</u> <u>think</u> <u>so</u>.

Teacher	Student
Do you think it will rain today? I think so.	I think so.
Do you think Fran will win the race? I hope so.	I hope so.

Do you think Lee will pay for the tree?
Do you think Fran likes to run?
Do you hope that Fran will win the race?
Do you think that the firefighters will save Rose and Joe's house?
Do you think that Jill will be a good driver?

LISTENING COMPREHENSION

   If you have a fire, there are three things to think of:
First, get everyone away from the burning building fast.
Don't stop to telephone. Don't stop to take anything with you.
   Second, phone the fire department from next door or from
a pay phone.
   Third, never go back into a burning building.

---

1. Teacher reads the story twice at a normal pace.
   Student listens. Student asks about words he does not know.

2. Student tells the story in his own words. If the student cannot tell the
   story, teacher may begin the sentence and have the student complete it.

Note: If the student cannot remember the story, read it once or twice again.

ORAL EVALUATION

1. Using ESOL Illustrations 3, pp. 42-43, have the student identify sleepwear
   and bedding. Student should know all of the items.

2. Review the past participle of the irregular verbs by doing the drill on
   Answering Questions. Student should know all of the items.

3. Review hope + that clauses by doing the drill on Making Sentences.

4. Review so as a substitute by doing the Question and Answer Drill.

II. Reading and Writing

SKILL BOOK 3: Lesson 17

Complete Lesson 17 in Skill Book 3, following the instructions given in the
Laubach Way to Reading Teacher's Manual for Skill Book 3. Adapt the wording of
the suggested teacher's instructions to the student as needed for your ESOL
student's comprehension.

ADDITIONAL WRITTEN PRACTICE

After completing Lesson 17 in the skill book, have the student do the practices
for Lesson 17 in the Workbook for Skill Book 3.

Lesson 18

OBJECTIVES

When a student completes this unit, he should be able to:

1. Say and respond to a new dialog.
2. Say the words map and way.
3. Say some geographical terms.
4. Say some expressions of place.
5. Say the names of the four seasons.
6. Say some words about cooking appliances.
7. Say some words about catching cold.
8. Say some action verbs: load, lift, push, pull, drop.
9. Use which in questions.
10. Use questions with Would you mind + verb-ing.
11. Answer questions with Would you mind?
12. Use spend + time expressions + verb-ing.
13. Listen to a story and repeat it in his own words.

VISUAL AIDS

1. ESOL Illustrations 3, pp. 44-47.
2. The maps on p. 99 and p. 121 of Skill Book 3.
3. A globe or world map.
4. Any of these items that it is convenient to bring: a toaster, a frying pan, a can and can opener, a coffee pot, a teapot.

I. Conversation Skills

DIALOG

A: Would you mind opening the door for me?
   My hands are full.
B: I'll be glad to.
   Can I help you with your packages?

A: Thank you.
   Would you take this box and put it on the table?
B: Sure.

VOCABULARY: map and way

Look at the map to find Valley Road.
Look at the map to find the way to Green Lake State Park.

Use the map on p. 99 of Skill Book 3.

VOCABULARY: Geographical Terms

Ed is standing on the bank of the river.
Jill is standing on the shore of the lake.
Tom is standing on the shore of the ocean.

There is sand at the ocean.
Children play in the sand.
They like a sandy beach.

There is an island in the lake.
There are islands in the ocean.
Cuba is an island.

Use ESOL Illustrations 3, pp. 44-45, for the first seven sentences.
Use a globe or world map to point to islands in the ocean.
Use the map on p. 121 of Skill Book 3 or a globe or world map to show Cuba.

DRILL: Identification Drill

Using the visual aids listed above for the geographical terms, ask
questions to elicit the vocabulary items.

VOCABULARY: Expressions of Place

This is the front of the book.
This is the middle of the book.
This is the end of the book.

Use a book to show the meaning of the expressions.

DRILL: Identification Drill

Using the visual aids listed above for the geographical terms, ask questions to
elicit the vocabulary items.

<u>VOCABULARY</u>: The Four Seasons

There are four <u>seasons</u> in the year.
In the <u>winter</u>, it is cold. People go skiing.
In the <u>spring</u>, the trees are green. People go fishing.
In the <u>summer</u>, it is warm. People go swimming.
In the <u>fall</u>, the leaves of the trees get yellow and red.

<u>DRILL</u>: Answering Questions

Teacher asks questions to elicit the vocabulary.

<u>Teacher</u>	<u>Student</u>
How many seasons are there? There are four seasons.	There are four seasons.
When is it cold? It is cold in the winter.	It is cold in the winter.

When are the trees green?
When is it warm?
When is it cold?
When do the leaves of the trees get yellow and red?
How many seasons are there?

<u>VOCABULARY</u>: Cooking Appliances

Joan <u>toasts</u> bread in the <u>toaster</u>.
Joan <u>roasts</u> meat in the <u>oven</u>.
Joan <u>bakes</u> a cake in the <u>oven</u>.
Joan <u>boils</u> water on top of the <u>stove</u>.
Joan <u>fries</u> fish in a <u>frying pan</u>.
She opens a can with a <u>can opener</u>.
She makes coffee in a <u>coffee pot</u>.
She makes tea in a <u>teapot</u>.

Use <u>ESOL Illustrations 3</u>, pp. 46-47, or actual objects.

VOCABULARY: Catching Cold

People <u>catch</u> <u>cold</u> in the winter.
When a <u>person</u> has a cold, he has a <u>sore</u> <u>throat</u>.
He <u>sneezes</u> a lot and has to <u>blow</u> <u>his</u> <u>nose</u>.
He <u>needs</u> to drink a lot of water.
He needs to <u>rest</u> in bed.

Act out the meaning of the new vocabulary items.

DRILL: Answering Questions

Teacher asks questions which elicit the vocabulary items. As necessary, act out items to elicit responses (e.g., sneezing, blowing his nose).

Teacher	Student
What do people catch in the winter? They catch cold.	They catch cold.
When a person has a cold, what does he do? (Teacher sneezes.) He sneezes.	He sneezes.
When a person has a cold, what does he do? (Teacher blows her nose.)	
When a person has a cold, what does he have? (Teacher touches her throat and looks uncomfortable.)	
When a person has a cold, what does he need to drink? When a person has a cold, what does he need to do?	

VOCABULARY: Action Verbs

Tom puts boxes in the trunk. He <u>loads</u> the trunk.
He <u>lifts</u> the boxes up.
The box is heavy. He <u>drops</u> it.
He <u>pushes</u> the door shut.
He <u>pulls</u> the door open.

Act out the meaning of the verbs.

DRILL: Answering Questions

Teacher acts out the verbs and asks, "What am I doing?" For example, teacher lifts something and asks, "What am I doing?" Continue with the remaining items.

<u>STRUCTURE FOCUS</u>: <u>Questions with Which</u>

<u>Which</u> dress did you buy?   The blue one.
<u>Which</u> road are you going to take? The shore road.
<u>Which</u> book did you read?   The English book.
<u>Which</u> coat did you wear?   The black one.

---

1. Teacher models each question and answer, asking the student to listen to <u>which</u>. Student listens.

2. Teacher models each question and answer. Student repeats after each sentence.

<u>DRILL</u>: <u>Making Questions</u>

Teacher gives a statement, which the student must put in the question form.

<u>Teacher</u>	<u>Student</u>
I bought a blue dress. Which dress did you buy?	Which dress did you buy?
I put the brown bag in the car. Which bag did you put in the car?	Which bag did you put in the car?

She is taking Valley Road.
Ann is reading the English book.
Sam is wearing his black coat.
I bought the blue dress.
They went to Green Lake State Park.
Lee is going to take Flight 406.
Mike packed his black tie.
I put the brown bag in the car.

STRUCTURE FOCUS: <u>Would you mind</u> + <u>Verb-ing</u>

> <u>Would</u> <u>you</u> <u>mind</u> <u>closing</u> the door?
> <u>Would</u> <u>you</u> <u>mind</u> <u>opening</u> the window?
> <u>Would</u> <u>you</u> <u>mind</u> <u>putting</u> the bags in the trunk?

As you model each sentence, ask the student to listen to <u>Would you mind?</u>

DRILL: Making Questions

Teacher gives words which the student must use in the question form with <u>Would you mind</u>. Student completes the question.

<u>Teacher</u>	<u>Student</u>
close the window	
Would you mind closing the window?	Would you mind closing the window?
go by bus	
Would you mind going by bus?	Would you mind going by bus?

close the window
open the door
give me the book on the table
help me fill out this application
bring a green salad to the party
carry these books for me
put the bags in the trunk

STRUCTURE FOCUS: Answers to Would you mind?

Would you mind closing the window?
Not at all.

Would you mind helping me?
I'd be glad to.

Would you mind bringing a green salad to the party?
I'm sorry, but I'm not going to the party.

---

1. Teacher models each question and answer, asking the student to listen to the answer. Student listens.

2. Teacher models each question and answer. Student repeats the answer.

DRILL: Question and Answer Drill

Teacher asks a question which the student answers using an appropriate reply. Student replies may vary.

Teacher	Student
Would you mind going by bus? I'm sorry, but I can't.	I'm sorry, but I can't.
Would you mind helping me? I'd be glad to.	I'd be glad to.

Would you mind putting the bags in the trunk?
Would you mind giving me the book on the table?
Would you mind going by bus?
Would you mind carrying these books for me?
Would you mind helping me fill out this application?
Would you mind closing the window?
Would you mind closing the door?

STRUCTURE FOCUS: <u>spend</u> + <u>Time Expressions</u> + <u>Verb-ing</u>

Joan and her mother	spent	the day	fishing.
I	spent	two hours	studying.
Mrs. Oak	spent	an hour	making dinner.

As you model each sentence, ask the student to listen to <u>spent</u>.

DRILL: Combining Sentences

Teacher gives two sentences which the student must combine into one sentence.

<u>Teacher</u>   <u>Student</u>

I spent two hours.
I studied English.
I spent two hours studying English.   I spent two hours studying English.

Ed spent the day.
He worked.
Ed spent the day working.   Ed spent the day working.

Joan and her mother spent the day.
They fished.

The two men spent a lot of time.
They talked.

Joan spent the weekend.
She camped.

Mrs. Oak spent an hour.
She made dinner.

I spent two hours.
I watched TV.

I spent all my time.
I listened to the radio.

I spent two hours.
I studied English.

Ed spent the day.
He worked.

LISTENING COMPREHENSION

When you go camping in October, you need to take many things
with you. You need a tent and a sleeping bag. You need bread and
cheese. You can take coffee to drink. You can go fishing and roast
the fish over a fire.

Sometimes, it's cold in October, and it rains. You need heavy
clothes and a heavy coat.

---

1. Teacher reads the story twice at a normal pace.
   Student listens. Student asks about words he does not know.

2. Student tells the story in his own words. If the student cannot tell the
   story, teacher may begin the sentence and have the student complete it.

Note: If the student cannot remember the story, read it once or twice again.

ORAL EVALUATION

1. Using ESOL Illustrations 3, pp. 44-45, and a globe or world map, have the
   student identify the geographical terms. Student should know 5 of them.
2. Have the student identify the four seasons using the drill on Answering
   Questions.
3. Using ESOL Illustrations 3, pp. 46-47, have the student identify names of the
   cooking appliances. Student should know 8 of them.
4. Review the vocabulary on catching a cold by doing Answering Questions Drill.
5. Review the action verbs by doing the drill on Answering Questions. Student
   should know 4 of them.
6. Review questions with which by doing the drill on Making Questions.
7. Review questions with Would you mind? by doing the drill on Making Questions.
8. Review polite replies to Would you mind? by doing the Question and Answer
   Drill.
9. Review spend + time expressions + verb-ing by doing the drill on Combining
   Sentences.

II. Reading and Writing

SKILL BOOK 3: Lesson 18

Complete Lesson 18 in Skill Book 3, following the instructions given in the
Laubach Way to Reading Teacher's Manual for Skill Book 3. Adapt the wording of
the suggested teacher's instructions to the student as needed for your ESOL
student's comprehension.

ADDITIONAL WRITTEN PRACTICE

After completing Lesson 18 in the skill book, have the student do the practices
for Lesson 18 in the Workbook for Skill Book 3.

Lesson 19

OBJECTIVES

When a student completes this unit, he should be able to:

1. Say and respond to a new dialog.
2. Say some chart and story words about things that happen on the road.
3. Say some words about the weather.
4. Say the words ahead and behind.
5. Say the expression back and forth.
6. Say the irregular verbs blow, know, and throw.
7. Use had better.
8. Use so + adjective + that clause, as in It's so dark outside that I can't see.
9. Listen to a story and repeat it in his own words.

VISUAL AIDS

1. ESOL Illustrations 3, pp. 48-49.
2. An outdoor thermometer (Fahrenheit).

I. Conversation Skills

DIALOG

A: It's so cold. It's freezing out today.
B: Yes, it's five below zero.

A: And it's windy. That makes it seem colder.
B: Do you like the cold weather?

A: Yes, I do. And I like the snow, too.
B: Why?

A: Because I want to go skiing.
B: That's my favorite winter sport, too.

Use ESOL Illustrations 3, p. 48.

VOCABULARY: On the Road

The first car leads the way.
The second car follows.
The cars drive at the speed limit.
The speed limit is 55 miles an hour.
It is against the law to drive faster than the speed limit.

VOCABULARY: Weather and Temperatures

When it's zero outside, it's cold.
When it's below zero, it's very cold.
When it's eighty outside, it's warm.
When it's above eighty, it's very warm.
When it's thirty-two outside, water freezes. It changes to ice.

Use the thermometer in ESOL Illustrations 3, p. 49, or a real thermometer
to show the temperature in each sentence.

VOCABULARY: ahead and behind

Ed is in front of us. He is ahead.
Joan is in back of us. She is behind.

VOCABULARY: back and forth

She rocked back and forth.
The man rocked the car back and forth.
He goes back and forth to work by car.

Demonstrate the meaning of back and forth as you model the sentences.

VOCABULARY: Irregular Verb Forms

blow	blew	have blown
know	knew	have known
throw	threw	have thrown

1. Teacher models all three forms of each verb. Student listens.
2. Teacher models all three forms of each verb. Student repeats.

Note: Act out the meaning of blow and throw. For example, throw away some paper.

DRILL: Answering Questions

Teacher asks a questions which the student answers in the affirmative.

Teacher

Did the wind blow hard?
Yes, it blew hard.

Have you thrown the paper away?
Yes, I have thrown it away.

Does the wind blow snow onto the car windows?
Did he know what to say?
Did Ed throw the paper away?
Has he known Gail for a long time?
Has the wind blown the snow onto the car windows?
Does Sam know how to drive in the snow?
Did the wind blow hard yesterday?

Student

Yes, it blew hard.

Yes, I have thrown it away.

STRUCTURE FOCUS: The Use of had better

    I had better take some medicine.   I feel sick.
    I'd better take some medicine.   I feel sick.

    You had better wear a heavy coat. It's cold.
    You'd better wear a heavy coat.   It's cold.

    They had better not drive fast.   It's against the law.
    They'd better not drive fast.   It's against the law.

As you model each pair of sentences, ask the student to listen to had better, then I'd better, and so on.

DRILL: Making Sentences

Teacher gives words which the student must use in sentences beginning with You'd better.

Teacher

take some medicine
You'd better take some medicine.

study hard
You'd better study hard.

wear a heavy coat
drive slowly
not smoke in bed
telephone the police
not drive without a license
take some medicine
study hard

Student

You'd better take some medicine.

You'd better study hard.

STRUCTURE FOCUS: <u>so</u> + <u>Adjective</u> + <u>that</u> <u>Clause</u>

This box is <u>so</u> <u>heavy</u> <u>that</u> I can't carry it.
I'm <u>so</u> <u>angry</u> <u>that</u> I could yell.
Ed speaks <u>so</u> <u>softly</u> <u>that</u> I can't hear him.

As you model each sentence, ask the student to listen to <u>so...that</u>.

<u>Note</u>: The construction <u>so...that</u> is used with an adjective or adverb.

DRILL: <u>Combining Sentences</u>

Teacher gives two sentences which the student combines using <u>so...that</u>.

<u>Teacher</u>	<u>Student</u>

This box is heavy.
I can't carry it.
    This box is so heavy that
    I can't carry it.
	This box is so heavy that
	I can't carry it.

It's snowing hard.
Sam cannot see the road.
    It's snowing so hard that
    Sam cannot see the road.
	It's snowing so hard that
	Sam cannot see the road.

It's dark outside. I can't see.	
It's snowing hard. Sam cannot see the road.	
He's going fast. He will miss the turn.	
This sweater is expensive. I can't buy it.	
He's talking softly. I can't hear him.	
Joan is sad. She wants to cry.	
I am angry. I want to yell.	
This box is heavy. I can't carry it.	

LISTENING COMPREHENSION

It is not easy to drive when it is snowing and the wind is blowing. You must drive slowly in the snow. You must clean the ice and snow from your car windows. It's good to have a bag of sand and a blanket in your car. You can throw sand under the car wheels if your car gets stuck.

---

1. Teacher reads the story twice at a normal pace.
   Student listens. Student asks about words he does not know.

2. Student tells the story in his own words. If the student cannot tell the story, teacher may begin the sentence and have the student complete it.

Note: If the student cannot remember the story, read it once or twice again.

ORAL EVALUATION

1. Have the student say the words about things that happen on the road. He should know all of them.

2. Have the student say the words about weather and temperatures. He should know all of them.

3. Act out the words and have the student say ahead, behind, back and forth.

4. Review the irregular verbs by having the student do the drill on Answering Questions. Student should be able to answer all the questions.

5. Review had better by having the student do the drill on Making Sentences.

6. Review so + adjective + that clause by having the student do the drill on Combining Sentences.

II. Reading and Writing

SKILL BOOK 3: Lesson 19

Complete Lesson 19 in Skill Book 3, following the instructions given in the Laubach Way to Reading Teacher's Manual for Skill Book 3. Adapt the wording of the suggested teacher's instructions to the student as needed for your ESOL student's comprehension.

ADDITIONAL WRITTEN PRACTICE

After completing Lesson 19 in the skill book, have the student do the practices for Lesson 19 in the Workbook for Skill Book 3.

Lesson 20

<u>OBJECTIVES</u>

When a student completes this unit, he should be able to:

1. Say and respond to a new dialog.
2. Say vocabulary about clothing.
3. Say the word <u>directory</u> and recognize what a telephone directory and a store directory are.
4. Use the irregular verbs <u>tear</u>, <u>wear</u>, <u>swear</u>.
5. Use words about location: <u>across the street</u>, <u>on the corner</u>, and <u>next to</u>.
6. Use the expression <u>can afford to</u>.
7. Use the superlative form of adjectives.
8. Use <u>each other</u>.
9. Use <u>every other</u>, as in <u>every other day</u>.
10. Listen to a story and repeat it in his own words.

<u>VISUAL AIDS</u>

1. <u>ESOL</u> <u>Illustrations</u> <u>3</u>, pp. 50-51.
2. Lined writing paper.
3. A calendar for any month.
4. A telephone directory.

<u>I. Conversation Skills</u>

<u>DIALOG</u>

A: Could you tell me where I can find the men's department?
B: I'm sorry. I don't know.
   Let's look at the store directory.

A: Where is it?
B: On the first floor, near the door.

A: Oh, I see it.
   Men's Department. Fourth Floor.
   Thanks for your help.
B: Sure. Any time.

VOCABULARY: Clothing

David and Joan went to a department store.
David wanted a sport shirt with short sleeves.
Joan wanted a blouse with long sleeves.
David wanted a sweater, and Joan did, too.
A salesperson in the men's department showed David
    some shirts and sweaters.
A salesperson in the women's department showed Joan
    some blouses and sweaters.

Use ESOL Illustrations 3, p. 50, to show the clothing.

DRILL: Question and Answer Drill

Teacher asks questions to elicit vocabulary items.

Teacher	Student
What did the salesperson show David? The salesperson showed David some shirts.	The salesperson showed David some shirts.
What did Joan want? She wanted a blouse with long sleeves.	She wanted a blouse with long sleeves.
What did David want? What did the salesperson show David? What did Joan want? What did the salesperson show Joan?	

VOCABULARY: A Directory

A store directory is a sign.
It tells where to find things in a department store.

A telephone directory is a book.
It has people's telephone numbers in it.

Use ESOL Illustrations 3, top of p. 51, to show a store directory in a department store. Show the student the telephone directory you have brought, and point out your own name and number, or the student's, or some other listing that would be meaningful to him.

VOCABULARY: <u>Irregular Verb Forms</u>

tear	tore	torn
wear	wore	worn
swear	swore	sworn

1. Teacher models all three forms of each verb. Student listens.
2. Teacher models all three forms of each verb. Student repeats.

<u>Note</u>: Explain the meaning of the verbs by <u>tearing</u> a piece of paper, making a sentence about some article of clothing you <u>wear</u>, and holding up your hand as if taking an oath for <u>swear</u>.

DRILL: <u>Answering Questions</u>

Teacher asks a question which the student answers in the affirmative.

Teacher	Student
What did she wear?	
She wore a white blouse.	She wore a white blouse.
What did she tear?	
She tore some paper.	She tore some paper.

Has she worn that blouse before?
Do you wear hats?
Has he ever torn his shirt?
What did you swear to do?
What did Sam tear?
Have you ever sworn to do something?

VOCABULARY: <u>Expressions of Location</u>

The bookstore is <u>on the corner of</u> York Street and Main Street.
The bookstore is <u>across the street from</u> the post office.
The bank is <u>next to</u> the post office.

Use the map on the bottom of p. 51, <u>ESOL Illustrations 3</u>, to indicate the locations.

After modeling the sentences and having the student repeat, ask questions with "Where is ...?" to elicit <u>on the corner of</u>, <u>across the street from</u>, and <u>next to</u>.

<u>VOCABULARY</u>: <u>in order</u> and <u>out of order</u>

Steve fixed the TV.   It's <u>in order</u>.
The radio is broken.   It's <u>out of order</u>.

<u>VOCABULARY</u>: <u>can afford to</u>

I have enough money.   I <u>can afford to</u> buy these shoes.
I don't have enough money.   I <u>can't afford to</u> buy this car.

As you model each pair of sentences, ask the student to listen to <u>can afford to</u> or <u>can't afford to</u>.

<u>DRILL</u>: <u>Making Statements</u>

Teacher asks student to tell what he can afford to buy and what he cannot afford to buy. Teacher may begin by telling what she can and cannot afford and having the student repeat these statements.

<u>Teacher</u>	<u>Student</u>
I can afford to buy an English book.	I can afford to buy an English book.
I can't afford to buy a new car.	I can't afford to buy a new car.

What can you afford?
What else can you afford?

What can't you afford?
What else can't you afford?

STRUCTURE FOCUS: Superlatives of Adjectives

He looked at three shirts. He wanted <u>the cheapest one</u>.
The yellow shirt was the <u>best</u> shirt.
The best shirt cost the <u>most</u> money.

As you model each sentence, ask the student to listen to <u>the cheapest</u>,
<u>the best</u>, and <u>the most</u>.

DRILL: Making Questions

Teacher gives words which the student must use with <u>Which is</u> to form a question.

Teacher	Student
the cheapest shirt	
Which is the cheapest shirt?	Which is the cheapest shirt?
the most expensive blouse	
Which is the most expensive blouse?	Which is the most expensive blouse?
the most money	
the most expensive blouse	
the cheapest shirt	
the best blouse	
the cleanest room	
the best cake	

STRUCTURE FOCUS: The Use of each other

We write to each other every week.
They see each other every day.
Ann and I telephone each other every morning.

As you model each sentence, ask the student to listen to each other.

DRILL: Making Sentences

Teacher gives words which the student must use in a sentence with each other.

Teacher   Student

Ann and I write
    Ann and I write to each other   Ann and I write to each other
    every week.   every week.

We ask
    We ask each other questions.   We ask each other questions.

We visit
They love
Gail and Jason love
We write
They see
Ann and I telephone

STRUCTURE FOCUS: The Use of every other

Please write on every other line.
He calls me every other day.
Every other street is one-way.

As you model each sentence, ask the student to listen to every other.
Use lined paper to demonstrate writing on every other line.
On a calendar, indicate every other day.

DRILL: Answering Questions

Teacher asks questions which the student must answer using every other.
Answers may vary.

Teacher	Student
When does he call you?	
He calls me every other day.	He calls me every other day.
When do you go camping?	
We go camping every other week.	We go camping every other week.
When does Ed write his mother?	
When does Gail go shopping?	
When does Sam call his friend?	
When does he write?	
When do you go camping?	
When do you go to the movies?	

LISTENING COMPREHENSION

Steve hurried into Porter's Department Store. He looked at the directory on the first floor. He wanted to buy a man's sport shirt. The directory said the men's department was on the fourth floor. Steve hurried to the fourth floor to look at sport shirts. He saw a nice yellow one that he liked very much. He bought it and left the store.

---

1. Teacher reads the story twice at a normal pace.
   Student listens. Student asks about words he does not know.

2. Student tells the story in his own words. If the student cannot tell the story, teacher may begin the sentence and have the student complete it.

Note: If the student cannot remember the story, read it once or twice again.

ORAL EVALUATION

1. Have the student do the Question and Answer Drill about clothing. He should be able to answer all the questions.

2. Review the irregular verbs by having the student do the drill on Answering Questions. Student should know all the verb forms.

3. Have the student make three or four sentences telling what he can or cannot afford to buy.

4. Review the superlatives by doing the drill on Making Questions.

5. Review each other by doing the drill on Making Sentences.

6. Review every other by doing the drill on Answering Questions.

II. Reading and Writing

SKILL BOOK 3: Lesson 20

Complete Lesson 20 in Skill Book 3, following the instructions given in the Laubach Way to Reading Teacher's Manual for Skill Book 3. Adapt the wording of the suggested teacher's instructions to the student as needed for your ESOL student's comprehension.

ADDITIONAL WRITTEN PRACTICE

After completing Lesson 20 in the skill book, have the student do the practices for Lesson 20 in the Workbook for Skill Book 3.

Lesson 21

OBJECTIVES

When a student completes this unit, he should be able to:

1. Say and respond to a new dialog.
2. Use the word instead.
3. Use the irregular verbs come, become, get, and forget.
4. Use vocabulary concerning schools.
5. Use as far as and until.
6. Use two-word verbs with up: drink up, eat up, finish up, and clean up.
7. Use but...anyway, as in She doesn't like TV, but she watches it anyway.
8. Use although clauses.
9. Listen to a story and repeat it in his own words.

VISUAL AIDS

None.

I. Conversation Skills

DIALOG

Gas station attendant:	May I help you?
Customer:	Yes, fill it up with unleaded gas.
Gas station attendant:	All right. Do you want me to check the oil?
Customer:	No, but could you clean my windows?
Gas station attendant:	Sure.
Customer:	How much do I owe you?
Gas station attendant:	Ten dollars, please.

Note: The dialog can be varied by substituting other items or services one can get at a gas station, such as air in tires.

<u>VOCABULARY</u>: The Use of <u>instead</u>

Joe wanted to smoke. He ate <u>instead</u>.
Mary wanted to go shopping. She studied <u>instead</u>.
Tom wanted to buy a yellow shirt. He got a blue one <u>instead</u>.

As you model each pair of sentences, ask the student to listen to <u>instead</u>.

<u>DRILL</u>: <u>Question and Answer Drill</u>

Teacher asks questions to elicit <u>instead</u>. Student replies may vary.

<u>Teacher</u>	<u>Student</u>
Tom wanted to go home. Where did he go instead? He went shopping instead.	He went shopping instead.
Tom wanted to buy a yellow shirt. What did he get instead? He got a blue shirt instead.	He got a blue shirt instead.
Joe wanted to smoke. What did he do instead?	
Ann wanted to go fishing. Where did she go instead?	
Joan wanted to study English. What did she study instead?	
Fran wanted to run. What did she do instead?	
Ann wanted to study. What did she do instead?	

VOCABULARY: Irregular Verb Forms

come	came	have come
become	became	have become
get	got	have gotten
forget	forgot	have forgotten

1. Teacher models all three forms of each verb. Student listens.
2. Teacher models all three forms of each verb. Student repeats.

DRILL: Answering Questions

Teacher asks a question which the student answers. Student replies may vary.

Teacher	Student
When does Ann come to class?	
She comes to class every day.	She comes to class every day.
What has Fran become?	
She has become a fast runner.	She has become a fast runner.

When did the police officers come to Tony's house?
Why did you come here?
What has Fran become?
What did Pete become?
What did Ed get?
When did you forget your book?
What have you forgotten?

VOCABULARY: Schools

Many people go to school.

Young children go to kindergarten first,
then to elementary school.

Teenagers go to junior high school,
then to high school.

After high school, many young people go
to a university or college.

Many adults go to school at night.

DRILL: Question and Answer Drill

Teacher asks questions to elicit vocabulary items.

Teacher	Student
Where do children go to school first? They go to kindergarten.	They go to kindergarten.
After kindergarten, where do children go to school? They go to elementary school.	They go to elementary school.

Who goes to school?
Where do children go to school first?
Where do children go after kindergarten?
Where do teenagers go to school?
After high school, where do many young people go to school?
When do many adults go to school?

VOCABULARY: <u>as far as</u> and <u>until</u>

He walked <u>as far as</u> the lake.
Ed came <u>as far as</u> the park.

He studied <u>until</u> 10 o'clock.
He lived in Canada <u>until</u> 1980.

As you model each sentence, ask the student to listen to <u>as far as</u> or <u>until</u>.

Note: <u>As far as</u> is used with a place, whereas <u>until</u> is used with a time.

DRILL: Question and Answer Drill

Teacher asks a question which the student answers using <u>as far as</u> or <u>until</u>. Student replies may vary.

Teacher	Student
How far did Tony walk?	
He walked as far as the lake.	He walked as far as the lake.
How long did Carla study?	
She studied until 10 o'clock.	She studied until 10 o'clock.
How far did Fran run?	
How far did Pete walk with you?	
How long did Rosa work?	
How long did Pete live in Canada?	
How long did Carla study English?	

VOCABULARY: Two-Word Verbs with up

Drink up your milk. Don't leave any in the glass.
Eat up your meat. Don't leave any on the plate.
Finish up your homework. Do all the homework.
Clean up your room. Don't leave it dirty.
---

1. Teacher models each pair of sentences, asking the student to listen to drink up, eat up, finish up, and clean up. Student listens.

2. Teacher models the sentence. Student repeats after each sentence.

Note: The use of up emphasizes doing the action to its final point.

DRILL: Making Sentences

Teacher gives words or phrases which the student uses in statements with drink up, eat up, finish up, and clean up. Student replies may vary.

Teacher	Student
your room	
Clean up your room.	Clean up your room.
the letter	
Finish up the letter.	Finish up the letter.
the milk	
the meat on your plate	
your homework	
your room	
the kitchen	
this job	

STRUCTURE FOCUS: The Use of but...anyway

She doesn't like TV, <u>but</u> she watches it <u>anyway</u>.
It was raining, <u>but</u> they went camping <u>anyway</u>.
Steve was very busy, <u>but</u> he fixed Mrs. Green's radio <u>anyway</u>.

As you model each sentence, ask the student to listen to <u>but</u>...<u>anyway</u>.

DRILL: Combining Sentences

Teacher gives sentences which the student combines using <u>but</u>...<u>anyway</u>.

Teacher	Student
She doesn't like TV.	
She watches it.	
She doesn't like TV,	She doesn't like TV,
but she watches it anyway.	but she watches it anyway.
There was ice on the road.	
He drove fast.	
There was ice on the road,	There was ice on the road,
but he drove fast anyway.	but he drove fast anyway.
It was raining.	
They went camping.	
This coat is old.	
I'm going to wear it.	
It's late.	
I'm going to call Joan.	
Meat is expensive.	
We buy it.	
Steve was busy.	
He fixed Mrs. Green's radio.	
Steve tore his shirt.	
He wore it.	
He should study.	
He is going to the movies.	

STRUCTURE FOCUS: <u>Although Clauses</u>

         Although she was tired, she went to work.
         Although it was cold, Tony went fishing.
         Although it was late, Mrs. Green wasn't sleeping.

As you model each sentence, ask the student to listen to <u>although</u>.

DRILL: <u>Combining Sentences</u>

Teacher gives sentences which the student must combine using <u>although</u>.

<u>Teacher</u>	<u>Student</u>
Rose was tired.	
She went to work.	
Although Rose was tired,	Although Rose was tired,
she went to work.	she went to work.
The police tried hard.	
They didn't find Tony's sofa.	
Although the police tried hard,	Although the police tried hard,
they didn't find Tony's sofa.	they didn't find Tony's sofa.
Lee's car hit the tree.	
He did not get hurt.	
Rose was tired.	
She went to work.	
It was cold.	
Joan went swimming.	
Pete wanted to play hockey.	
He had to get another job.	
Steve was busy.	
He fixed the radio.	
It was late.	
Mrs. Green wasn't sleeping.	

LISTENING COMPREHENSION

Many people enjoy shopping. They like to go shopping
on the weekends. They go in many stores to see what is for
sale. They go shopping for clothes, for furniture, and for
many other things. Although people can't afford to buy
everything they want, they have fun looking at the things
in the stores. And they buy what they can afford.

---

1. Teacher reads the story twice at a normal pace.
   Student listens. Student asks about words he does not know.

2. Student tells the story in his own words. If the student cannot tell the
   story, teacher may begin the sentence and have the student complete it.

Note: If the student cannot remember the story, read it once or twice again.

ORAL EVALUATION

1. Have the student do the Question and Answer Drill on instead.

2. Review the irregular verbs by doing the drill on Answering Questions.
   Student should know all of the verb forms.

3. Have the student do the Question and Answer Drill on schools.
   Student should be able to answer 4 out of 6 questions.

4. Have student distinguish between as far as and until by doing the Question
   and Answer Drill.

5. Have the student make sentences with the two-word verbs with up.
   Student should know all 4 verbs.

6. Have the student do the drill on Combining Sentences using but...anyway.

7. Have the student do the drill on Combining Sentences using although.

II. Reading and Writing

SKILL BOOK 3: Lesson 21

Complete Lesson 21 in Skill Book 3, following the instructions given in the
Laubach Way to Reading Teacher's Manual for Skill Book 3. Adapt the wording of
the suggested teacher's instructions to the student as needed for your ESOL
student's comprehension.

ADDITIONAL WRITTEN PRACTICE

After completing Lesson 21 in the skill book, have the student do the practices
for Lesson 21 in the Workbook for Skill Book 3.

Lesson 22

<u>OBJECTIVES</u>

When a student completes this unit, he should be able to:

1. Say and respond to a new dialog.
2. Use <u>wait on</u> and <u>wait for</u>.
3. Use some words about time: <u>present</u>, <u>past</u>, <u>future</u>.
4. Use some words about restaurants.
5. Name some musical instruments.
6. Use the word <u>union</u> in the sense of a labor union.
7. Use the words <u>citizen</u>, <u>immigrant</u>, and <u>refugee</u>.
8. Say the directions: <u>north</u>, <u>east</u>, <u>south</u>, and <u>west</u>.
9. Identify the directions on a map.
10. Say the names of some states and identify which part of the country (North, East, South, West) they are in.
11. Name some countries and people of North America.
12. Use <u>look forward to</u> + nouns.
13. Use <u>look forward to</u> + verb-<u>ing</u>.
14. Listen to a story and repeat it in his own words.

<u>VISUAL AIDS</u>

1. <u>ESOL</u> <u>Illustrations</u> <u>3</u>, pp. 52-53.
2. A calendar for a year.

I. Conversation Skills

<u>DIALOG</u>

> A: Do you like to listen to music?
> B: Yes, I like music.
>   I listen to music on the radio all the time.
>
> A: What kind of music do you like?
> B: I like fast music and some slow songs, too.
>
> A: Do you play in a band?
> B: No, I don't. I just like to listen.

<u>Note</u>: The dialog can be varied by discussing the kinds of music the student likes.

VOCABULARY: <u>wait on</u> and <u>wait for</u>

Rosa <u>waits</u> <u>on</u> tables at the snack shop.
The flight attendant <u>waits</u> <u>on</u> the passengers on the plane.

Ann is late. I'm <u>waiting</u> <u>for</u> her.
Ed is coming at 8 o'clock. We'll <u>wait</u> <u>for</u> him.

As you model the sentences, ask the student to listen to <u>wait</u> <u>on</u> and <u>wait</u> <u>for</u>.

Note: <u>Wait</u> <u>on</u> is used to mean "serve," whereas <u>wait</u> <u>for</u> means "to stay or remain until something happens."

DRILL: Question and Answer Drill

Teacher asks questions to elicit answers with <u>wait</u> <u>on</u> and <u>wait</u> <u>for</u>.

Teacher	Student
What does Rosa do at the snack shop?	
She waits on tables.	She waits on tables.
Ann is late. What are you going to do?	
I'm going to wait for her.	I'm going to wait for her.

The teacher isn't here yet. What are you going to do?
What does the flight attendant do?
What does the waiter do?
Ann is late. What are you going to do?
Hugo isn't here yet. What are you going to do?

VOCABULARY: Words about Time

Today is the <u>present</u>.
Yesterday was the <u>past</u>.
Tomorrow is the <u>future</u>.

DRILL: Answering Questions

Using a calendar, point to the day the class is in session. Say, "This is the present."

Point to other dates to elicit the sentences <u>This</u> <u>is</u> <u>the</u> <u>future</u> and <u>This</u> <u>is</u> <u>the</u> <u>past</u>. Conclude by pointing again to the present date to elicit <u>This</u> <u>is</u> <u>the</u> <u>present</u>.

VOCABULARY: Restaurants

Gail and Jason went to a restaurant for dinner.
They looked at the menu to see what to eat.

There were many desserts on the menu.
There was cake, apple pie, and ice cream.

There were many beverages on the menu.
There was milk, coffee, tea, and soda.

Use ESOL Illustrations 3, bottom of p. 52.

DRILL: Question and Answer Drill

Teacher asks questions to elicit vocabulary items.

Teacher	Student
Where did Gail and Jason go for dinner?	
They went to a restaurant.	They went to a restaurant.
What did they look at in the restaurant?	
They looked at the menu.	They looked at the menu.

Why did Gail and Jason look at the menu?
Where did Gail and Jason go for dinner?
What were some of the desserts on the menu?
What were some of the beverages on the menu?

VOCABULARY: Musical Instruments

Hugo plays in a band with other people.
Ann plays the piano.
Hugo plays the drums.
Ed plays the guitar.

Use ESOL Illustrations 3, bottom of p. 52.

DRILL: Identification Drill

Teacher points to the picture on p. 52 of ESOL Illustrations 3, and asks questions to elicit the vocabulary, such as: "What does Hugo play in?" "What's this?" and "What does ____ play?"

VOCABULARY: join a union

> Ed joined a union when he worked at a car factory.
> Hugo joined a union when he wanted to play in a band.
> Many people who work belong to unions.
> They are union members.

VOCABULARY: citizens, immigrants, and refugees

> The people of a country are its citizens.
> Immigrants are people who move into a new country to live.
> Refugees are people who leave their country because they are afraid.

VOCABULARY: Directions

> In the morning, the sun comes up in the east.
> In the afternoon, the sun is in the south.
> In the evening, the sun goes down in the west.
> The sun is never in the north.

As you model each sentence, ask the student to listen to east, south, and so on.
Point to the actual direction as you say each sentence. You may want to place
signs with these words on them around the room.

DRILL: Giving Answers

Teacher elicits the vocabulary. Point to the actual direction
for each item, and have the student point also.

Teacher	Student
Tell me where the sun comes up in the morning.	
The sun comes up in the east in the morning.	The sun comes up in the east in the morning.
Tell me where the sun is in the afternoon.	
The sun is in the south in the afternoon.	The sun is in the south in the afternoon.

Tell me where the sun comes up in the morning.
Tell me where the sun is in the afternoon.
Tell me where the sun goes down in the evening.
Tell me where the sun never is.

VOCABULARY: Directions on a Map

This is a map.
This is north.
This is east.
This is south.
This is west.

Use the map on p. 53 of ESOL Illustrations 3 to indicate the directions. After you have modeled the sentences and have had the student repeat, indicate the various directions, and have the student identify them.

VOCABULARY: States and Directions

This is a map of the United States.
There are 50 states in the United States.

New York is in the East.
Florida is in the South.
Texas is in the South.
California is in the West.
Minnesota is in the North.

Use the map on p. 53 of ESOL Illustrations 3 again.

DRILL: Question and Answer Drill

Teacher asks questions to elicit the vocabulary.

Teacher	Student
Where is New York?	
New York is in the East.	New York is in the East.
Where is Minnesota?	
Minnesota is in the North.	Minnesota is in the North.
Where is Texas?	
Where is California?	
Where is Minnesota?	
Where is Florida?	
Where is New York?	

VOCABULARY: Countries in North America

The United States, Mexico, and Canada are
big countries in <u>North</u> <u>America</u>.

Cuba is a small country in North America.

Cuba and Mexico are south of the United States.
Canada is north of the United States.
Mexico is west of Cuba.
Cuba is east of Mexico.

Use the map on p. 121 of <u>Skill</u> <u>Book</u> <u>3</u>.

DRILL: Answering Questions

Teacher asks questions to elicit vocabulary.
Use the map on p. 121 of <u>Skill</u> <u>Book</u> <u>3</u>.

Teacher	Student
Where is the United States? The United States is in North America.	The United States is in North America.
What are three big countries in North America? The United States, Mexico, and Canada are three big countries in North America.	The United States, Mexico, and Canada are three big countries in North America.

Where is Cuba?
Where is Canada?
Is Canada north of the United States?
Is Cuba west of Mexico?
Is Mexico west of Cuba?
What is a small country in North America?

VOCABULARY: Some People of North America

Americans live in the United States.
Mexicans live in Mexico.
Canadians live in Canada.
Cubans live in Cuba.

Use the map on p. 121 of Skill Book 3.

DRILL: Question and Answer Drill

Teacher asks questions to elicit vocabulary items.

Teacher	Student
Where is the United States?	
It is in North America.	It is in North America.
Who lives in the United States?	
Americans live in the United States.	Americans live in the United States.

Where is Mexico?
Who lives in Mexico?
Where is Canada?
Who lives in Canada?
Where is Cuba?
Who lives in Cuba?
Which is the biggest country in North America, Canada or the United States?
Which is bigger, Mexico or Cuba?

STRUCTURE FOCUS: look forward to + Noun

The Garcias look forward to a better future.
I'm looking forward to the party on Friday night.

As you model each sentence, ask the student to listen to look forward to.

DRILL: Answering Questions

Teacher gives a question and cue which the student must answer using look forward to + a noun.

Teacher   Student

What are you looking forward to?
(the party)
    I'm looking forward to the party.   I'm looking forward to the party.

What are the Garcias looking forward to?
(a better future)
    The Garcias are looking forward to   The Garcias are looking forward to
    a better future.   a better future.

What is Carla looking forward to?
(the class party)

What is Jill looking forward to?
(her birthday)

What is Fran looking forward to?
(the race)

What is David looking forward to?
(dinner with Carla)

What are the Garcias looking forward to?
(a better future)

What are you looking forward to?
(the party)

STRUCTURE FOCUS: <u>look forward to</u> + <u>Verb-ing</u>

```
    They          look   forward to   going home.
     I            look   forward to   seeing you again.
The Garcias   are looking forward to   becoming citizens.
```

As you model each sentence, ask the student to listen to <u>look forward to</u>.

DRILL: <u>Making Questions</u>

Teacher gives words which the student must use with <u>Are you looking forward to</u>
to form a question.

<u>Teacher</u>   <u>Student</u>

go to the party
    Are you looking forward to   Are you looking forward to
    going to the party?   going to the party?

see Gail and Jason again
    Are you looking forward to   Are you looking forward to
    seeing Gail and Jason again?   seeing Gail and Jason again?

get your driver's license
go to Mexico
become a citizen
learn to read English
go camping next weekend
play cards with the Masons

LISTENING COMPREHENSION

   The United States, Mexico, and Canada are three big countries
in North America, but Canada is the biggest of the three. Mexico
and Canada are neighbors of the United States.
   Many people in Canada speak English and French. Many people in
Mexico speak Spanish and English. Most people in the United States
speak English. Some speak a second language.

---

1. Teacher reads the story twice at a normal pace.
   Student listens. Student asks about words he does not know.

2. Student tells the story in his own words. If the student cannot tell the
   story, teacher may begin the sentence and have the student complete it.

<u>Note</u>: If the student cannot remember the story, read it once or twice again.

ORAL EVALUATION

1. Have the student do the drill for <u>wait</u> <u>on</u> and <u>wait</u> <u>for</u>.

2. Using a calendar, have the student make sentences using <u>present</u>, <u>past</u>, and <u>future</u>.

3. Have the student do the Question and Answer Drill on restaurants. Student should know all the items.

4. Using <u>ESOL</u> <u>Illustrations</u> <u>3</u>, p. 52, have the student identify the musical instruments. Also, ask, "What does Hugo play in?"

5. Using p. 53 of <u>ESOL</u> <u>Illustrations</u> <u>3</u>, have the student identify the directions on the map. Also, do the Question and Answer Drill on states and directions.

6. Using the map of p. 121 of <u>Skill</u> <u>Book</u> <u>3</u>, have the student identify some countries in North America and the names of the people of these countries.

7. Have the student review <u>look</u> <u>forward</u> <u>to</u> with nouns and with verb-<u>ing</u> by doing the two drills.

II. Reading and Writing

SKILL BOOK 3: Lesson 22

Complete Lesson 22 in <u>Skill</u> <u>Book</u> <u>3</u>, following the instructions given in the Laubach Way to Reading <u>Teacher's</u> <u>Manual</u> <u>for</u> <u>Skill</u> <u>Book</u> <u>3</u>. Adapt the wording of the suggested teacher's instructions to the student as needed for your ESOL student's comprehension.

ADDITIONAL WRITTEN PRACTICE

After completing Lesson 22 in the skill book, have the student do the practices for Lesson 22 in the <u>Workbook</u> <u>for</u> <u>Skill</u> <u>Book</u> <u>3</u>.

Lesson 23-A

Note: Lessons 23 and 24 are divided into A and B sections, as are Lessons 23 and 24 in Skill Book 3. Each section accompanies one story in the correlated reader Changes. Because the reading and writing portion of these lessons is very long, dialogs, listening comprehension, and oral evaluations are omitted from the conversation skills portions.

OBJECTIVES

When a student completes this unit, he should be able to:

1. Use the verb share.
2. Use the adjectives free, expensive, and cheap.
3. Use the verbs agree and disagree.
4. Use so + adjective + that clause (review).
5. Use wonder + if clause.

VISUAL AIDS

None.

I. Conversation Skills

VOCABULARY: The Verb share

> I pay half of the rent.
> Jason pays half of the rent.
> We share the cost of the rent.
>
> I did half of the work.
> Jason did half of the work.
> We shared the work.

---

1. Teacher models each group of sentences, asking the student to listen to share. Student listens.

2. Teacher models each group of sentences. Student repeats sentence with share.

VOCABULARY: free, expensive, cheap

This doesn't cost anything.   It's free.
This costs a lot of money.   It's expensive.
This doesn't cost much money. It's cheap.
---

1. Teacher models each pair of sentences. Student listens.
2. Teacher models each pair of sentences. Student repeats the sentence with the adjective.

DRILL: Rejoinder Drill

Teacher gives a statement to which the student adds a rejoinder with free, expensive, or cheap.

Teacher	Student
This doesn't cost anything. It's free.	It's free.
This costs a lot of money. This doesn't cost much money. This doesn't cost anything.	

VOCABULARY: The Verbs agree and disagree

I like music, but Jane doesn't. We disagree.
I like TV, and Jane does, too. We agree.

As you model the sentences, ask the student to listen to agree and disagree.

DRILL: Rejoinder Drill

Teacher tells about two people. Student must say whether they agree or disagree.

Teacher	Student
Jason likes ice cream, and Gail does, too. They agree.	They agree.
Jason likes cake, but Gail doesn't. They disagree.	They disagree.
I like to watch TV, and Gail does, too. Kay likes to play cards, and Ray does, too. Carla doesn't like diet soda, but David does. I like to visit Canada, and my friend does, too. Ann likes dogs, but the Smiths don't. Mike likes to fly, and Fran does, too.	

STRUCTURE FOCUS: Review of <u>so</u> + Adjective + <u>that</u> Clause

---

Jason was <u>so</u> <u>tired</u> <u>that</u> he went to sleep.
The dress was <u>so</u> <u>cheap</u> <u>that</u> I wanted it.
It was <u>so</u> <u>cold</u> <u>that</u> I put on my sweater.

As you model each sentence, ask the student to listen to <u>so</u>...<u>that</u>.

DRILL: Combining Sentences

Teacher gives two sentences which the student combines using <u>so</u>...<u>that</u>.

Teacher	Student

Jason was very tired.
He went to sleep.
    Jason was so tired that
    he went to sleep.
	Jason was so tired that
	he went to sleep.

The dress was very cheap.
I wanted it.
    The dress was so cheap that
    I wanted it.
	The dress was so cheap that
	I wanted it.

It was very cold. I put on my sweater.	
Jason was very busy. He didn't have time to spend with Gail.	
Fran is very sad. She is crying.	
Ed is very angry. He is shouting.	
David is very happy. He is smiling.	

STRUCTURE FOCUS: wonder + if Clause

> Jason wonders if he will be a good father.
> Gail wonders if she can afford a new dress.
> I wonder if it will rain this afternoon.

As you model each sentence, ask the student to listen to wonder if.

DRILL: Completing Sentences

Teacher begins a sentence which the student completes. Answers may vary.

Teacher	Student
I wonder if Gail	
I wonder if Gail will buy a new dress.	I wonder if Gail will buy a new dress.
I wonder if it	
I wonder if it will rain.	I wonder if it will rain.

Jason wonders if he
Gail wonders if she
I wonder if I
I wonder if it
Fran wonders if she
Lee Chan wonders if he

ORAL EVALUATION

1. Review the adjectives free, expensive, and cheap by doing the Rejoinder Drill.
2. Have the student do the Rejoinder Drill on agree and disagree.
3. Review so + adjective + that clause by doing the drill on Combining Sentences.
4. Review wonder + if clauses by doing the drill on Completing Sentences.

II. Reading and Writing

SKILL BOOK 3: Lesson 23-A

Complete Lesson 23-A in Skill Book 3, following the instructions given in the Laubach Way to Reading Teacher's Manual for Skill Book 3. Adapt the wording of the suggested teacher's instructions to the student as needed for your ESOL student's comprehension.

Note: In the Workbook for Skill Book 3, all of the exercises for Lesson 23 should be done following Lesson 23-B.

Lesson 23-B

When a student completes this unit, he should be able to:

1. Use some vocabulary about farm workers.
2. Say some adjectives and their opposites: <u>hard-working</u>, <u>lazy</u>, <u>friendly</u>, <u>unfriendly</u>, <u>lovely</u>, <u>handsome</u>, and <u>ugly</u>.
3. Use the verb <u>train</u>.
4. Use <u>no</u> as a modifier of nouns, as in <u>I</u> have <u>no money</u>, contrasted with contractions of <u>not</u>, as in <u>I</u> don't have any money.
5. Use clauses with <u>so that</u> to express purpose, as in <u>I must take classes so that I can get a better job</u>.
6. Use adjective clauses with <u>where</u> and <u>when</u>.

VISUAL AIDS

1. <u>ESOL Illustrations 3</u>, p. 54.
2. A piece of cotton cloth or some item made of cotton.

I. Conversation Skills

VOCABULARY: Farm Workers

Many farm workers are <u>migrant workers</u>.
The <u>migrants</u> go from one farm to another to work.
They pick the <u>crops</u> on the farm.
They pick <u>cotton</u>, peaches, beans, and other fruits and vegetables.

Use <u>ESOL Illustrations 3</u>, p. 54, which shows migrant workers picking cotton. Also, show the cotton item you brought to help explain the meaning.

VOCABULARY: Adjective Opposites

Carlos is hard-working. He works very hard.
Ed is lazy. He doesn't work very hard.

Carlos is friendly. He is nice to people.
Ed is unfriendly. He is not nice to people.

That woman is lovely. She looks pretty.
That man is handsome. He looks good, too.
That building is ugly. It looks bad.

As you model each group of sentences, ask the student to listen to hard-working, lazy, and so on. Have the student repeat the group of sentences.

DRILL: Answering Questions

Teacher asks questions which elicit the adjectives being taught.

Teacher	Student
What do we call a person who works hard? He's hard-working.	He's hard-working.
What do we call a building that looks bad? It's ugly.	It's ugly.
What do we call a person who is nice to people? What do we call a person who is not nice to people?	
What do we call a person who works hard? What do we call a person who doesn't work very hard?	
What do we call a woman who looks pretty? What do we call a man who looks good? What do we call a building that looks bad?	

VOCABULARY: The Verb <u>train</u>

Fran wants to win the mile race.
She has to <u>train</u> for the race.

Joan wants to be a nurse.
She has to <u>train</u> to become a nurse.

As you model each pair of sentences, ask the student to listen to <u>train</u>.

DRILL: Question and Answer Drill

Teacher asks questions which elicit the verb <u>train</u>.

Teacher	Student
What does Fran have to do to win the race? She has to train for the race.	She has to train for the race.
What does Joan have to do to become a nurse? She has to train to become a nurse.	She has to train to become a nurse.

What does Steve have to do to work in a repair shop?
What does Joan have to do to become a nurse?
What does Fran have to do to win the race?

STRUCTURE FOCUS: The Use of no + Nouns

> I have no money.
> He had no home of his own.
> There was no food in the house.

As you model each sentence, ask the student to listen to no.

DRILL: Transformation Drill

Teacher gives statements which the student must change using no + nouns.

Teacher   Student

I have money.
I have no money.   I have no money.

There is food in the kitchen.
There is no food in the kitchen.   There is no food in the kitchen.

He had a home of his own.
I need help.
There is a way to help him.
I have time.
They have money.

STRUCTURE FOCUS: <u>no</u> + <u>Nouns</u>, <u>not</u> + <u>Verbs</u>

I have <u>no</u> money.   I <u>don't</u> have any money.
There was <u>no</u> food. There <u>wasn't</u> any food.

---

1. Teacher models the sentences in pairs, the one with <u>no</u> and the one with <u>not</u> (contracted). Ask the student to listen to <u>no</u> and <u>not</u>.

2. Teacher models each pair of sentences. Student repeats after each sentence.

Note: While <u>no</u> is used before nouns, <u>not</u> is used to make a verb negative. It is often contracted.

DRILL: Transformation Drill

Teacher gives an affirmative sentence which the student must change in two ways to give a negative meaning: once with <u>no</u> and once with <u>not</u>.

Teacher   Student

Gail has some shampoo.
Gail has no shampoo.   Gail has no shampoo.
Gail doesn't have any shampoo.   Gail doesn't have any shampoo.

I have money.
I have no money.   I have no money.
I don't have any money.   I don't have any money.

Jason had lunch.
We have hamburger.
Carlos had a home of his own.
I had time to think.
I put sugar in the tea.
There is food in the kitchen.
There are vegetables in the refrigerator.
There was a way to help Ed.

STRUCTURE FOCUS: Clauses with <u>so that</u>

I must take classes <u>so that</u> I can get a better job.
She is learning to drive <u>so that</u> she can get a driver's license.

As you model each sentence, ask the student to listen to <u>so that</u>.

<u>Note</u>: <u>So that</u> is used in cause-and-effect clauses. It is often used with <u>can</u> to express ability.

DRILL: Combining Sentences

Teacher gives two sentences which the student combines using <u>so that</u>.

Teacher	Student
I must take classes.	
I can get a better job.	
I must take classes so that	I must take classes so that
I can get a better job.	I can get a better job.
Lee Chan is in the United States.	
He can go to the university.	
Lee Chan is in the United States	Lee Chan is in the United States
so that he can go to the university.	so that he can go to the university.

Fran runs every day.
She can win the mile race.

They are studying English.
They can get better jobs.

Lee Chan is in the United States.
He can go to the university.

She is learning how to drive.
She can get a driver's license.

They are coming to the United States.
They can have a better future.

STRUCTURE FOCUS: Adjective Clauses with where and when

The farm was 200 miles from the city where Carlos lived.
The building where he lives is in the city.

This is the day when I start my English class.
Monday is the day when I will see Hugo.

As you model each sentence, ask the student to listen to where or when.

DRILL: Combining Sentences

Teacher gives two sentences which the student must combine using where or when.

Teacher	Student

The farm was 200 miles from the city.
Carlos lived there.
    The farm was 200 miles from the city
    where Carlos lived.
	The farm was 200 miles from the city
	where Carlos lived.

Monday is the day.
I will see Jason then.
    Monday is the day
    when I will see Jason.
	Monday is the day
	when I will see Jason.

Carlos went to the farm. Maria was picking corn there.	
This is the city. I was born here.	
This is the bank. I keep my money here.	
Monday is the day. I will see Jason then.	
7:30 is the time. The plane will arrive then.	
Tomorrow is the day. I start my English classes then.	

ORAL EVALUATION

1. Review the adjective opposites by doing the drill on Answering Questions. Student should know all of the adjectives.

2. Review _no_ and _not_ by doing the Transformation Drill.

3. Review _so that_ by doing the drill on Combining Sentences.

4. Review adjective clauses with _where_ and _when_ by doing the drill on Combining Sentences.

II. Reading and Writing

SKILL BOOK 3: Lesson 23-B

Complete Lesson 23-B in _Skill Book 3_, following the instructions given in the Laubach Way to Reading _Teacher's Manual for Skill Book 3_. Adapt the wording of the suggested teacher's instructions to the student as needed for your ESOL student's comprehension.

ADDITIONAL WRITTEN PRACTICE

After completing Lesson 23-B in the skill book, have the student do the practices for Lesson 23 in the _Workbook for Skill Book 3_.

Lesson 24-A

<u>OBJECTIVES</u>

When a student completes this unit, he should be able to:

1. Say vocabulary about the handicapped.
2. Use the words <u>wild</u> and <u>tame</u>.
3. Use the word <u>nearly</u>.
4. Say the vocabulary about Braille.
5. Use the verb <u>trust</u>.
6. Use the verbs of the senses: <u>see</u>, <u>hear</u>, <u>smell</u>, <u>feel</u>, <u>taste</u>.
7. Use <u>able</u> + infinitive, as in <u>She is able to see</u>.

<u>VISUAL AIDS</u>

<u>Changes</u>, p. 21.

<u>I. Conversation Skills</u>

<u>VOCABULARY</u>: <u>The Handicapped</u>

A <u>blind</u> person cannot see.
A <u>deaf</u> person cannot hear.
These people are <u>handicapped</u>. They have <u>handicaps</u>.
There are other kinds of handicaps.
Some people get a handicap after a <u>sickness</u>.

<u>DRILL</u>: <u>Question and Answer Drill</u>

Teacher asks questions to elicit the vocabulary items.

<u>Teacher</u>	<u>Student</u>
Who cannot see? A blind person cannot see.	A blind person cannot see.
Who cannot hear? A deaf person cannot hear.	A deaf person cannot hear.

When do some people become handicapped?
What handicaps do some people have?
Who cannot see?
Who cannot hear?

VOCABULARY: <u>wild</u> <u>and</u> <u>tame</u>

      Some animals in the woods are <u>wild</u>.
      Dogs and cats are <u>tame</u>.

VOCABULARY: The Use of <u>nearly</u>

      Anne Sullivan was <u>nearly</u> blind when she was a girl.
      It's <u>nearly</u> 7:30 p.m.

As you model each sentence, ask the student to listen to <u>nearly</u>.
Explain that <u>nearly</u> means the same as <u>almost</u>.

DRILL: Expansion Drill

Teacher gives a sentence which the student repeats, adding <u>nearly</u>.

Teacher	Student
It's 7:30.	
It's nearly 7:30.	It's nearly 7:30.
I am 35.	
I am nearly 35.	I am nearly 35.

I'm ready.
It's time to stop.
It's October.
It's 10 o'clock.
The movie is over.
Anne Sullivan was blind when she was a girl.

VOCABULARY: <u>Braille</u>

      Blind people learn how to read <u>Braille</u>.
      <u>Braille</u> is a way of writing with <u>raised</u> <u>dots</u>.
      Blind people <u>touch</u> the raised dots with their fingers.

Use the picture on p. 21 of <u>Changes</u> to help explain the meaning of the words.

VOCABULARY: The Verb <u>trust</u>

Helen Keller believed in Anne Sullivan.
Helen was not afraid.
She <u>trusted</u> Anne.

VOCABULARY: Verbs of the Senses

We <u>see</u> with our eyes.
We <u>hear</u> with our ears.
We <u>smell</u> with our nose.
We <u>feel</u> with our hands.
We <u>taste</u> with our tongue.

As you model each sentence, act out the meaning of the verb.

VOCABULARY: Past Tense of Verbs of the Senses

We <u>saw</u> his car yesterday.
We <u>heard</u> the music last night.
We <u>smelled</u> the cake in the oven.
We <u>felt</u> the Braille.
We <u>tasted</u> the cake.

DRILL: Transformation Drill

Teacher gives a statement in the present tense which the student transforms into the past tense.

Teacher	Student
I see his car now.	
I saw his car yesterday.	I saw his car yesterday.
We hear the music.	
We heard the music.	We heard the music.
We smell the bread.	
Helen feels the Braille.	
We taste the bread.	
She sees the boy.	
I hear something in the kitchen.	

STRUCTURE FOCUS: <u>be</u> + <u>able</u> + <u>Infinitive</u>

I can hear you very well.
I <u>am</u> <u>able</u> <u>to</u> <u>hear</u> you very well.

I can't see the blackboard.
I <u>am</u> <u>not</u> <u>able</u> <u>to</u> <u>see</u> the blackboard.

Can you see the blackboard?
<u>Are</u> you <u>able</u> <u>to</u> <u>see</u> the blackboard?

---

1. Teacher models each pair of sentences, asking the student to listen to <u>able</u> <u>to</u>. Student listens. Explain that <u>able</u> <u>to</u> means <u>can</u>.

2. Teacher models each pair of sentences. Student repeats only the sentence with <u>able</u> <u>to</u>.

<u>Note</u>: <u>Able</u> means "having the ability" to do something. <u>Can</u> often expresses the same meaning, but it may also be used to express the meaning of "having the right" or "having the permission" to do something, as in <u>Can</u> <u>we</u> <u>park</u> <u>here?</u>

DRILL: <u>Transformation Drill</u>

Teacher gives a sentence with <u>can</u> which the student changes into a sentence with <u>able</u> <u>to</u>.

<u>Teacher</u>	<u>Student</u>
I can't come to the party. I'm not able to come to the party.	I'm not able to come to the party.
Can he walk without help? Is he able to walk without help?	Is he able to walk without help?
Can she fly an airplane? A cat can see in the dark. I can't answer that question. Can he run fast? He can't work full time. Can you see the blackboard? I can't see the blackboard. I can hear you very well.	

STRUCTURE FOCUS: Past Tense with able

Carla <u>was</u> <u>able</u> <u>to</u> <u>finish</u> her homework quickly last night.
Joe Stone <u>was</u> <u>able</u> <u>to</u> <u>quit</u> smoking in a few months.

Mr. and Mrs. Hunt <u>were</u> <u>not</u> <u>able</u> <u>to</u> <u>go</u> to sleep.
Helen Keller <u>was</u> <u>not</u> <u>able</u> <u>to</u> <u>hear</u> <u>or</u> <u>speak</u>.

As you model each sentence, ask the student to listen to <u>was</u> <u>able</u> <u>to</u> or <u>were</u> <u>able</u> <u>to</u>.

DRILL: Expansion Drill

Teacher gives words which the student uses in a negative past tense statement with <u>I</u> <u>was</u> <u>not</u> <u>able</u> <u>to</u>.

Teacher   Student

go to sleep
I was not able to go to sleep.   I was not able to go to sleep.

lift that heavy box
I was not able to lift that heavy box.   I was not able to lift that heavy box.

finish my homework
go to the concert
hear what she was saying
save any money
find a cheap car
wait for you
go to sleep
lift that heavy box

STRUCTURE FOCUS: Future Tense with able

I <u>will</u> <u>be</u> <u>able</u> <u>to</u> <u>help</u> you tomorrow.
Carlos <u>will</u> <u>not</u> <u>be</u> <u>able</u> <u>to</u> <u>save</u> any money next month.
<u>Will</u> you <u>be</u> <u>able</u> <u>to</u> <u>finish</u> your work by five o'clock?

As you model each sentence, ask the student to listen to <u>will</u> <u>be</u> <u>able</u> <u>to</u>.

DRILL: Making Sentences

Teacher gives a <u>when</u> clause and a phrase. Student uses these in a sentence with <u>will</u> <u>be</u> <u>able</u> <u>to</u> in the main clause.

Teacher	Student
When Carlos gets a better job... buy a car 　　When Carlos gets a better job, 　　he will be able to buy a car.	When Carlos gets a better job, he will be able to buy a car.
When it snows... go skiing 　　When it snows, 　　we will be able to go skiing.	When it snows, we will be able to go skiing.
When spring comes... play baseball	
When I finish doing the dishes... help you with your homework	
When Jill is 16... get a driver's license	
When the weekend comes... sleep later	
When Carlos gets a better job... buy a car	
When it snows... go skiing	

ORAL EVALUATION

1. Review vocabulary about the handicapped by doing the Question and Answer Drill. Student should know all the items.

2. Review the use of <u>nearly</u> by doing the Expansion Drill.

3. Review the past tense of verbs of the senses by doing the Transformation Drill.

4. Review <u>be</u> + <u>able</u> + infinitive by doing the Transformation Drill.

5. Review the past tense with <u>able</u> by doing the Expansion Drill.

6. Review the future tense with <u>able</u> by doing the drill on Making Sentences.

II. Reading and Writing

SKILL BOOK 3: Lesson 24-a

Complete Lesson 24-a in <u>Skill</u> <u>Book</u> <u>3</u>, following the instructions given in the Laubach Way to Reading <u>Teacher's</u> <u>Manual</u> <u>for</u> <u>Skill</u> <u>Book</u> <u>3</u>. Adapt the wording of the suggested teacher's instructions to the student as needed for your ESOL student's comprehension.

<u>Note</u>: In the <u>Workbook</u> <u>for</u> <u>Skill</u> <u>Book</u> <u>3</u>, all of the exercises for Lesson 24 should be done following Lesson 24-B.

Lesson 24-B

<u>OBJECTIVES</u>

When a student completes this unit, he should be able to:

1. Say some adjectives and related abstract nouns, such as <u>free</u> and <u>freedom</u>.
2. Say some words about civil rights.
3. Say some words about protests.
4. Use the word <u>boycott</u>.
5. Say some words about the Nobel Peace Prize.
6. Say the names of some cities in Alabama and its state capital, and recognize Washington, D.C., as the capital of the United States.

<u>VISUAL AIDS</u>

1. <u>ESOL Illustrations 3</u>, pp. 55-56.
2. <u>Changes</u>, p. 27.

<u>I. Conversation Skills</u>

<u>VOCABULARY</u>: <u>Adjectives and Abstract Nouns</u>

---

1. There is <u>beauty</u> in the sky and trees.
   These things are <u>beautiful</u>.

2. Martin Luther King had <u>courage</u>.
   He was not afraid. He was <u>brave</u>.
   He wanted <u>justice</u> for his people.
   He wanted all people to be <u>fair</u> to his people.

3. Martin Luther King did not want <u>violence</u>.
   He did not want people to be hurt.
   He did not want people to be <u>violent</u>.

4. Martin Luther King wanted <u>equality</u> for his people.
   He wanted his people to be the same as all other people.
   He wanted everyone to be <u>equal</u>.

5. Martin Luther King wanted <u>freedom</u> for his people.
   He wanted all people to be <u>free</u> and have their <u>rights</u>.

---

1. Teacher models the sentences in groups, as numbered. Student listens.
2. Teacher models the sentences. Student repeats after each sentence.

VOCABULARY: Civil Rights

People have the right to say what they want.
People have the right to go to any church they want.
People have the right to go to any meetings they want.
These are some of the civil rights that people in the United States have.
The United States cannot make a law to take away these civil rights.

---

1. Teacher says each sentence, asking the student to listen to right or civil rights. Student listens.

2. Teacher models the sentences. Student repeats after each sentence.

3. Teacher asks the student to tell some of the civil rights that people in the United States have.

VOCABULARY: Protests

When people's civil rights are taken away, they protest.
When people protest, they march together.
These people are protesters.
People who walk together to protest are marchers.

Martin Luther King was a leader.
He led protesters in a march.
He was put in jail.
He was arrested by the police and put in jail.

Use the pictures on pp. 27 and 28 of Changes that show Dr. King in jail and leading a protest to help the student understand this vocabulary.

DRILL: Answering Questions

Using the pictures in Changes, ask the student questions to elicit the vocabulary about protests, such as:

Where is Dr. King? (in jail)
What is Martin Luther King doing in this picture? (leading a march)
Who are the people in the picture? (protesters)
What are the people in the picture doing? (protesting)

VOCABULARY: boycott

The black ministers planned a bus boycott.
They asked people to stop riding the city buses.

Explain that a boycott is a way of protesting. In a boycott, people stop buying or using something.

VOCABULARY: <u>The Nobel Prize</u>

Martin Luther King was a good leader.
He won a big <u>prize</u>.
He won the <u>Nobel</u> <u>Peace</u> <u>Prize</u> for leading
    the non-violent protests for civil rights.

As you model the sentences, ask the student to listen to the words <u>Nobel</u> <u>Peace</u> <u>Prize</u>. Use the photo of on p. 55 of <u>ESOL</u> <u>Illustrations</u> <u>3</u>.

VOCABULARY: <u>Cities and Capitals</u>

<u>Alabama</u> is a state in the South.
<u>Selma</u> and <u>Birmingham</u> are cities in Alabama.
<u>Montgomery</u> is another city in Alabama.
Montgomery is the <u>capital</u> of Alabama. It is the state capital.

<u>Washington</u>, <u>D.C.</u>, is a city in the East.
It is the <u>capital</u> of the United States.

Use the United States map on p. 53 of <u>ESOL</u> <u>Illustrations</u> <u>3</u> to locate Alabama in the South and to show Washington, D.C. Use the map of Alabama on p. 56 to show the cities in Alabama.

<u>Note</u>: You may also want to teach the capital of your state and mark it on the map on p. 53.

DRILL: <u>Answering Questions</u>

Using the two maps, ask questions which elicit the vocabulary items, such as:

Where is Montgomery?
What is the capital of Alabama?
Where is Alabama?
What is Washington, D.C.?
Where is Selma?
What are three cities in Alabama?
Is Alabama a city or a state?
Is Washington, D.C. a city or a state?
Where is Birmingham?

ORAL EVALUATION

Review the new vocabulary as needed by having the student repeat the sentences or by using the drills provided.

II. Reading and Writing

SKILL BOOK 3: Lesson 24-B

Complete Lesson 24-B in Skill Book 3, following the instructions given in the Laubach Way to Reading Teacher's Manual for Skill Book 3. Adapt the wording of the suggested teacher's instructions to the student as needed for your ESOL student's comprehension.

ADDITIONAL WRITTEN PRACTICE

After completing Lesson 24-B in the skill book, have the student do the practices for Lesson 24 in the Workbook for Skill Book 3.

Oral Evaluation for Skill Book 3

This Oral Evaluation covers the material introduced in the Conversation Skills. It is divided into two parts. Part I is a review of 75 vocabulary items, grouped according to topic. Part II is a review of the basic structural patterns taught, grouped according to patterns.

PART I. VOCABULARY

Procedure: The 75 vocabulary items in this part appear in the Teacher's Evaluation Form which follows. To conduct this part of the Oral Evaluation, follow the directions below for each set of items.

Items 1-4:   Use p. 4 of ESOL Illustrations for Skill Book 3. Elicit the names of the food items pictured. You may begin by saying: "When Mrs. Falco goes to the supermarket to buy food, what does she buy?"

Items 5-9:   Use pp. 5-6 of ESOL Illustrations for Skill Book 3. Have the student identify vegetables. You may ask: "What's this?" or "What are these?"

Items 10-14:   Use pp. 10-13 of ESOL Illustrations for Skill Book 3. Elicit play or go plus the activity being pictured. You may ask: "What are they doing?"

Items 15-20:   Use pp. 14-15 of ESOL Illustrations for Skill Book 3. Ask the student to identify some basic tools and equipment. You may ask: "What's this?"

Items 21-25:   Use p. 16 of ESOL Illustrations for Skill Book 3. Ask the student to identify parts of the face. You may say: "Carla has a pretty face," and then ask, "What is this?" or "What are these?"

Items 26-27:   Use p. 20 of ESOL Illustrations for Skill Book 3. Elicit the activity picture. You may ask: "What is this person doing?"

Items 28-34:   Use pp. 21-23 of ESOL Illustrations for Skill Book 3. Ask the student to name some items of personal grooming. You may ask: "What do you wash your face with?" and so on, pointing to the items as necessary.

Items 35-38:   Student should respond with an appropriate adjective as you ask:

35. How do we feel when a friend yells at us?
36. How do we feel when a friend gets sick?
37. How do we feel when a friend gets better?
38. How does Mrs. Green feel when her son comes home late?

Items 39-43:   The student should give the adjective opposite to the one you use. To begin, say: "I say the book is big. You say the opposite--the book is small." Then use the cues below.

39. Beans are cheap. Meat is ____.
40. The day is bright. The night is ____.
41. The big building is high. The small building is ____.
42. His hands are dirty. My hands are ____.
43. This book is open. That one is ____.

Items 44-48:   Use p. 27 of <u>ESOL</u> <u>Illustrations</u> <u>for</u> <u>Skill</u> <u>Book</u> <u>3</u>. Elicit the
               prepositions. You may ask: "Where is Ray sitting?" and so on.

Items 49-53:   Use pp. 30-31 of <u>ESOL</u> <u>Illustrations</u> <u>for</u> <u>Skill</u> <u>Book</u> <u>3</u>. Elicit names
               of items used for cleaning. You may say: "When Steve cleans the
               shop, he uses many things. What are these things?" Then, point to
               each item.

Items 54-58:   Elicit verbs about feelings. You may ask the questions below. You
               may also need to act out the verbs.

               54. What does Fran do when something is funny?
               55. What does Fran do when she is happy?
               56. What does Fran do when she is not happy?
               57. What does Fran do when she is very sad?
               58. What does Fran do when she is angry?

Items 59-61:   Elicit the irregular plurals. You may say: "I have one knife; you
               have two ____," and so on.

Items 62-64:   Use pp. 40-41 of <u>ESOL</u> <u>Illustrations</u> <u>for</u> <u>Skill</u> <u>Book</u> <u>3</u>. Elicit names
               of public employees. You may ask: "Who is this?"

Items 65-68:   Elicit the names of the seasons. You may ask:

               65. What season is very hot? People go swimming then.
               66. In what season do the leaves of the trees get red and
                   yellow?
               67. In what season do the trees get green?
               68. What season is very cold?

Items 69-72:   Elicit names of schools. You may ask:

               69. Where do young children go to school first?
               70. Where do they go after kindergarten?
          71-72. Where do teenagers go to school?

Items 73-75:   You may ask:

               73. What do you call the people of a country?
               74. What do you call people who move into a new country to live?
               75. What do you call people who leave their country because they
                   are afraid?

<u>Scoring</u>: Assess your student's performance and check the appropriate column on
the Teacher's Evaluation Form.

-- Check column 1 if the student identifies the item fairly quickly and with
   fairly understandable pronunciation.

-- Check column 2 if the student identifies the item with some hesitation but
   with fairly understandable pronunciation.

-- Check column 3 if the student identifies the picture incorrectly, or if,
   after a short wait, he cannot identify it at all.

No matter how the student answers, do not tell him he is right or wrong. Do not
look disappointed or disapproving if he gives you an incorrect answer or does
not answer at all. Go on briskly with the evaluation.

PART I. VOCABULARY: Teacher's Evaluation Form

Student's name _____ Date _____

1	2	3		1	2	3	
__	__	__	1. ham	__	__	__	39. expensive
__	__	__	2. hamburger	__	__	__	40. dark
__	__	__	3. beans	__	__	__	41. low
__	__	__	4. tea	__	__	__	42. clean
				__	__	__	43. shut
__	__	__	5. tomatoes				
__	__	__	6. lettuce	__	__	__	44. between
__	__	__	7. carrots	__	__	__	45. next to
__	__	__	8. potatoes	__	__	__	46. in back of
__	__	__	9. onions	__	__	__	47. in front of
				__	__	__	48. in the back of
__	__	__	10. play cards				
__	__	__	11. play football	__	__	__	49. broom
__	__	__	12. play hockey	__	__	__	50. dustpan
__	__	__	13. go swimming	__	__	__	51. mop
__	__	__	14. go skiing	__	__	__	52. vacuum cleaner
				__	__	__	53. sponge
__	__	__	15. hammer				
__	__	__	16. screwdriver	__	__	__	54. laugh
__	__	__	17. saw	__	__	__	55. smile
__	__	__	18. scissors	__	__	__	56. frown
__	__	__	19. ladder	__	__	__	57. cry
__	__	__	20. pail	__	__	__	58. shout
				__	__	__	59. knives
__	__	__	21. hair	__	__	__	60. feet
__	__	__	22. lips	__	__	__	61. children
__	__	__	23. cheeks				
__	__	__	24. teeth	__	__	__	62. police officer
__	__	__	25. ears	__	__	__	63. firefighter
				__	__	__	64. mail carrier
__	__	__	26. take a bath				
__	__	__	27. take a shower	__	__	__	65. summer
				__	__	__	66. fall
__	__	__	28. soap	__	__	__	67. spring
__	__	__	29. towel	__	__	__	68. winter
__	__	__	30. washcloth				
__	__	__	31. toothbrush	__	__	__	69. kindergarten
__	__	__	32. razor	__	__	__	70. elementary school
__	__	__	33. shampoo	__	__	__	71. junior high school
__	__	__	34. comb	__	__	__	72. high school
__	__	__	35. angry	__	__	__	73. citizens
__	__	__	36. sad	__	__	__	74. immigrants
__	__	__	37. glad	__	__	__	75. refugees
__	__	__	38. upset				
				__	__	__	Part I Totals

Procedure: In this part, the student is asked to produce the major structural patterns that have been taught. The 75 items in this part are listed below. They are grouped in sets according to structural patterns.

In each set of items, there are two examples for you to use to show the student what is expected of him. Say both the teacher's cue and the expected student response. Have the student repeat the response after you.

For the remaining (numbered) items in the set, give only the cues. Do not prompt the student or help him. If he seems confused, simply repeat the two examples given, having him repeat the responses after you. If he cannot do one set, proceed briskly to the next one without showing signs of disapproval or discouragement.

SET A: Past Tense with Irregular Verbs

Teacher's cue	Student response
What did you send your mother?	I sent her a letter.
When did Ed cut the grass?	He cut it yesterday.

1. What did David lend Tom?
2. Who cut the bread?
3. How much did Jason spend?
4. Where did Ed sleep?
5. What did Carla give the baby?
6. Who did Mr. Chan speak to?
7. Who did Mr. Chan shake hands with?
8. When did Kim break the dish?
9. What did the man steal?
10. What color coat did Gail choose?

SET B: Questions in the Present Perfect Tense

Teacher's cue	Student response
She painted a house.	Has she ever painted a house?
She washed the dog.	Has she ever washed the dog?

11. He slept on the floor.
12. Ed spent a lot of money.
13. She sang the song.
14. Carla gave him some money.
15. Jason ate all the cake.
16. David swept the kitchen.
17. Gail kept the money.
18. Mr. Oliver lived in New York City.
19. Fran ran in the race.
20. Mr. Chan shook the teacher's hand.

SET C: Statements in the Passive Voice

Teacher's cue	Student response
Someone steals the ring.	The ring is stolen.
Someone broke the lock.	The lock was broken.

21. Someone wrote this book.
22. Someone steals the book.
23. Someone drove the truck.
24. People speak English in many countries.
25. People read the book in English.

SET D: Reflexive Pronouns

Teacher's cue	Student response
Who stopped the washing machine?	It stopped itself.
Who are we buying the books for?	We are buying them for ourselves.

26. Who hurt the cat?
27. Who was I talking to?
28. Who is David buying the shirt for?
29. Who are they getting the books for?
30. Who is Carla baking the cake for?

SET E: Verbs + Gerunds or Infinitives

Teacher's cue	Student response
I'll learn	I'll learn to read.
I've finished	I've finished working.

31. She'll plan
32. He has quit
33. I'll tell her
34. Jason stopped
35. He wants
36. He has practiced
37. It takes 30 minutes
38. I'm tired of
39. Lee is worried about
40. It's time

SET F: Sequence of Tenses in Clauses

Teacher's cue	Student response
We'll see if	We'll see if Ellen can help us.
I could speak Italian when	I could speak Italian when I was a child.

41. When Carla calls
42. I can't tell if
43. When the telephone rings
44. I'll ask Ann if
45. When the teacher talked

<u>SET G</u>: <u>Short Answers to Questions</u>

<u>Teacher's cue</u>	<u>Student response</u>
Is Ann in class?	No, she isn't.
Did Fran go running yesterday?	Yes, she did.

46. Could she help you?
47. Will you drive me home, please?
48. Has Fran been running for a year?
49. Can Jason fix the stairs?
50. Should Tom smoke so much?
51. Are you able to see the blackboard?
52. Would you mind closing the window?

<u>SET H</u>: <u>Short Answers to Questions</u>

<u>Teacher's cue</u>	<u>Student response</u>
Fran and Mike are retired	Fran and Mike are retired, aren't they?
You had better wear a heavy coat	You had better wear a heavy coat, hadn't you?

53. You wouldn't mind helping me
54. People don't go fishing in the river
55. You can't see the church from here
56. Mr. Chan has met his teacher
57. Carla can speak English
58. The police didn't find the ring
59. Tom hasn't ever played soccer
60. They will play hockey in Canada

<u>SET I</u>: <u>Adjective Clauses with</u> <u>that</u>

<u>Teacher's cue</u>	<u>Student response</u>
I like the frame.	
Gail put the picture in it.	I like the frame that Gail put the picture in.
Lee went to see the tree.	
He hit the tree.	Lee went to see the tree that he hit.

61. You can keep the money. Mrs. Green gave you the money.
62. They painted the apartment. They lived in the apartment.
63. Ann goes to a class. The class meets in a church.
64. Ray and Kay are going to a movie. The movie is about a little girl.
65. He can read the book. I gave him the book.

SET J: Statements with but...anyway

Teacher's cue   Student response

There was ice on the road.
He drove fast.   There was ice on the road, but he drove fast anyway.

Steve tore his shirt.
He wore it.   Steve tore his shirt, but he wore it anyway.

66. It was raining. They went camping.
67. This dress is old. I'm going to wear it.
68. It's late. I'm going to call Joan.

SET K: Statements with as...as

Teacher's cue   Student response

Pete is sad. Lee is sad.   Pete is as sad as Lee.
Fran ran fast. Kim ran fast.   Fran ran as fast as Kim.

69. Lee Chan speaks slowly. I speak slowly.
70. Jane's hair is dark. Gail's hair is dark.
71. Mrs. Green is worried. Lee is worried.

SET L: Verbs with Prepositions

Teacher's cue   Student response

Ed--afraid--dogs   Ed is afraid of dogs.
Mrs. Green--angry--Lee   Mrs. Green is angry at Lee.

72. Pete--worried--mother
73. Carla--right--the price of the book
74. We--tired--television
75. I--interested--this book

Scoring: Assess your student's performance and check the appropriate column on the Teacher's Evaluation Form that follows. Evaluate the student's performance on a scale of 1 to 3, using the same criteria as for the vocabulary:

-- Check column 1 if the student gives the correct structure, responding fairly quickly and with fairly understandable pronunciation.

-- Check column 2 if the student gives the correct structure with some hesitation but with fairly understandable pronunciation.

-- Check column 3 if the student cannot form the structure correctly or if, after a short wait, he cannot respond at all.

Evaluate only the structure in question. For example, suppose the student is asked to change a statement into a question in the present perfect tense. After the cue "Mr. Oliver lived in New York City," he says: "Has Mr. Oliver ever lived in New York?" responding fairly quickly and with good pronunciation. In such a case, check column 1 even though the student has omitted the word City. He has formed the question correctly in the present perfect tense, and that is the structure in question.

PART II. STRUCTURAL PATTERNS: Teacher's Evaluation Form

Student name _____ Date _____

		1	2	3				1	2	3
Set A	1.	___	___	___		Set F	41.	___	___	___
	2.	___	___	___			42.	___	___	___
	3.	___	___	___			43.	___	___	___
	4.	___	___	___			44.	___	___	___
	5.	___	___	___			45.	___	___	___
	6.	___	___	___						
	7.	___	___	___		Set G	46.	___	___	___
	8.	___	___	___			47.	___	___	___
	9.	___	___	___			48.	___	___	___
	10.	___	___	___			49.	___	___	___
							50.	___	___	___
Set B	11.	___	___	___			51.	___	___	___
	12.	___	___	___			52.	___	___	___
	13.	___	___	___						
	14.	___	___	___		Set H	53.	___	___	___
	15.	___	___	___			54.	___	___	___
	16.	___	___	___			55.	___	___	___
	17.	___	___	___			56.	___	___	___
	18.	___	___	___			57.	___	___	___
	19.	___	___	___			58.	___	___	___
	20.	___	___	___			59.	___	___	___
							60.	___	___	___
Set C	21.	___	___	___						
	22.	___	___	___		Set I	61.	___	___	___
	23.	___	___	___			62.	___	___	___
	24.	___	___	___			63.	___	___	___
	25.	___	___	___			64.	___	___	___
							65.	___	___	___
Set D	26.	___	___	___						
	27.	___	___	___		Set J	66.	___	___	___
	28.	___	___	___			67.	___	___	___
	29.	___	___	___			68.	___	___	___
	30.	___	___	___						
						Set K	69.	___	___	___
Set E	31.	___	___	___			70.	___	___	___
	32.	___	___	___			71.	___	___	___
	33.	___	___	___						
	34.	___	___	___		Set L	72.	___	___	___
	35.	___	___	___			73.	___	___	___
	36.	___	___	___			74.	___	___	___
	37.	___	___	___			75.	___	___	___
	39.	___	___	___						
	40.	___	___	___						

Part II Totals ___ ___ ___

EVALUATING THE STUDENT'S PERFORMANCE

Part I. Vocabulary

If your student gets a total of 60 or more checks in columns 1 and 2, he is ready to begin Skill Book 4.

You should, however, look over the vocabulary items he missed and review them, a few at a time, in subsequent lessons.

If your student gets a total of 45-59 checks in columns 1 and 2, you must spend some time reviewing the vocabulary items he missed before beginning Skill Book 4.

Anything less than 44 checks in columns 1 and 2 indicates need for extensive review before beginning Skill Book 4.

Always combine review of vocabulary with review of structural patterns. For example, if the student was unable to name any of the tools, combine a review of those items with a review of question and answer patterns.

Part II. Structural Patterns

If your student gets a total of 60 or more checks in columns 1 and 2, he is ready to begin Skill Book 4.

It is important, however, that you analyze the items he missed. If he missed most or all of the items in a section, be sure to review that structural pattern again before beginning Skill Book 4.

If your student gets less than 60 in columns 1 and 2, it is especially important to review any basic structures he is having difficulty with before beginning Skill Book 4.

Review only those structures that caused the most difficulty. If a student missed only one item in a section, review would generally not be necessary. Watch for sections in which the student missed most or all of the items, and review those structures in particular. In general, the more checks in column 3 in a particular section, the more time you will need to spend reviewing that structure.

Note: The publisher hereby grants permission to reproduce the Teacher's Evaluation Forms for Parts I and II for the purpose of evaluating student performance.

Conversation Skills Word List

Words that appear in the list below are items introduced in the Vocabulary and Structure Focus sections of this manual. Items are listed only when the student himself is asked to produce them. Items that occur only in the Dialogs are not listed. The numbers refer to lesson numbers, not pages.

The main entries are the normal dictionary-entry forms, including irregular verb forms. Examples of usage and structures are listed under the main entries. A dash indicates that the main-entry word is taught only in the expression given below it. Variants formed by adding endings to root words are not listed.

Underlined listings refer to categories of words that are introduced as a group. (The underlined words themselves are not part of the student's vocabulary, however, unless they are listed elsewhere.)

24-A	able	8	in the back of
19	above	19	back and forth
9	account	15	back up
10	adult	5	bake
20	afford	10	Baker (family name)
14	afraid	8	banana
1	after	22	band (music)
7	again	9	bank
19	against	18	bank (of the river)
11	age	3	baseball
23-A	agree	3	basketball
19	ahead	18	beach
7	air	1	beans
24-B	Alabama	24-B	beautiful
15	almost	24-B	beauty
5	already	21	became
21	although	14	because
13	a.m.	21	become
22	Americans	17	Bedding
7	angry	1	beef
1	animals	12	been
5	any more	1	before
8	anyone	19	behind
8	anything	19	below
--	anyway	8	best
21	but...anyway	15	better
11	application	19	had better
10	appointment	22	beverages
24-B	arrest	7	Beverages
14	arrive	1	bill
14	as...as	24-B	Birmingham
21	as far as	11	birth
2	baby-sits	11	birthday
2	baby-sitter	17	blanket
7	back	19	blew
8	in back of	24-A	blind

20	blouse	23-B	cotton
19	blow	16	could
18	blow one's nose	16	couldn't
19	blown	10	countries
18	boil (v.)	24-B	courage
11	born	1	cow
16	both	24-A	crippled
24-B	boycott	23-B	crops
24-A	Braille	18	Cuba
24-B	brave	22	Cubans
16	break	2	cup
10	take a break	1	cut (past tense)
7	bright	10	Dallas
16	bring	--	date
16	broke	11	date of birth
16	broken	10	make a date
9	broom	1	David
4	brush	13	day
21	but...anyway	24-A	deaf
5	cake	14	depart
22	California	20	department
3	call	22	dessert
21	came	13	die
5	camera	20	directory
18	can opener	9	dirt
10	Canada	7	dirty
22	Canadians	23-A	disagree
24-B	capital	24-A	dots
3	cards	21	drink up
1	Carla	16	driven
23-B	Carlos	7	driver
2	carrots	16	drove
18	catch cold	12	drugstore
13	cemetery	22	drums
20	cheapest	5	drunk (past participle)
3	check	9	dustpan
4	cheeks	8	each
1	chicken	20	each other
16	choose	4	ears
16	chose	22	east
16	chosen	3	easy
22	citizens	21	eat up
24-B	civil rights	5	eaten
7	clean	9	eighteenth
21	clean up	9	eighth
9	cleaner	9	eightieth
2	clerk	21	elementary school
4	climb	9	eleventh
18	coffee pot	13	Ellen
18	cold (have a cold)	18	end of
21	college	24-B	equal
6	comb	24-B	equality
21	come (past participle)	20	every other
18	cook	8	everyone
18	Cooking Appliances	8	everything
1	cost	5	expensive

4	eyes	14	gate (at airport)
4	face	4	get
24-B	fair (adj.)	5	given
1	Falco (family name)	7	glad
18	fall	5	got
15	farther	21	gotten
23-B	Farm Workers	8	grape
12	feet	13	grave
7	felt	22	guitar
11	female	19	had better
9	fifteenth	4	hair
9	fifth	6	hairbrush
9	fiftieth	6	hairdryer
5	film	2	half
15	fine (a fine man)	1	ham
5	finish	1	hamburger
21	finish up	4	hammer
16	firefighter	24-A	handicap
13	flight	24-A	handicapped
13	flight attendant	3	hard (difficult)
22	Florida	23-B	hard-working
13	fly (v.)	5	hasn't
19	follow	5	haven't
1	food	3	have to
1	Food Items	2	head (of lettuce)
12	foot (measurement)	5	herself
3	football	4	high
5	forgave	21	high school
21	forget	5	himself
5	forgive	3	hockey
5	forgiven	17	hope
21	forgot	13	hour
21	forgotten	22	Hugo
9	fortieth	9	hundredth
15	forward	7	ice
9	fourteenth	7	iced
9	fourth	11	if
5	frame	22	immigrants
23-A	free	12	inch
24-B	freedom	10	infant
16	freeze	21	instead
23-B	friendly	14	interested
7	front	4	invite
8	in front of	18	island
8	in the front of	2	it (impersonal)
12	frown	5	itself
16	froze	5	I've
16	frozen	24-B	jail
8	fruit	5	Jane
18	fry	1	Jason
18	frying pan	18	Joan
2	full-time	17	Joe
13	funeral	22	join
22	future	21	junior high
4	Gail	24-B	justice
22	Garcia (family name)	2	Kay

15	leaves (n. pl.)	24-A	nearly
24-B	led	8	next to
6	Lee	3	nice
8	lemon	17	nightgown
1	lend	9	nineteenth
1	lent	9	ninetieth
15	less	9	ninth
1	lettuce	23-B	no (modifier)
11	license	8	no one
11	license plate	24-B	Nobel Peace Prize
4	lips	22	north
--	little (amount)	22	North America
15	I have little money.	8	nothing
18	load (v.)	9	Numbers, Ordinal
15	loaves	18	Oak (family name)
22	look forward to	18	ocean
1	Lopez (family name)	16	Oh
7	low	16	Oh, no!
23-B	lovely	16	Oh, well
16	mail carriers	2	onions
11	male	7	open (adj.)
18	map	8	orange
24-B	march	5	ourselves
24-B	marcher	4	order (v.)
3	Mason (family name)	20	out of order
17	mattress	20	in order
5	may (for permission)	7	outdoors
7	mean	18	oven
7	meant	3	paid
12	Measures, Length	4	pail
2	Measures, Liquid	4	paint
1	meat	17	pajamas
10	medicine	2	part-time
22	member	9	parts
22	menu	4	Parts of the Face
10	mess	7	passenger
22	Mexicans	22	past (time expression)
22	Mexico	2	pat (of butter)
18	middle	3	payday
23-B	migrant	24-B	peace
12	Mike	8	peach
12	mile	8	pear
--	mind	2	peas
18	Would you mind...?	6	Personal Grooming
13	minister	9	Pete
22	Minnesota	22	piano
13	minute	22	pie
10	mistake	1	pig
24-B	Montgomery	17	pillow
9	mop	13	pilot
10	more	--	pity
20	most	13	What a pity!
1	music	4	places
11	must	5	plate
5	myself	3	play (v.)
4	nails	4	pliers

13	p.m.	4	scissors
16	police officer	4	screwdriver
1	pork	4	screws
20	Porter (family name)	18	seasons
2	potato	7	seat
2	pound of	9	second (2nd)
13	pray	13	seconds (in a minute)
22	present (time expression)	24-B	Selma
1	price	1	sent
12	print (v.)	13	services
24-B	prize	9	seventeenth
24-B	protest	9	seventh
24-B	protester	9	seventieth
18	pull	11	sex
18	push	17	shaken
1	put (past tense)	4	shall
2	Quantities, Food in	--	shame
2	quarter (of a cup)	13	That's a shame!
5	quit	6	shampoo
12	race	23-A	share
24-A	raised	17	sheets
2	Ray	15	shelf
6	razor	15	shelves
22	refugees	17	shook
4	remember	18	shore (n.)
3	rent	14	should
9	repair	14	shouldn't
18	rest (v.)	12	shout
22	restaurant	6	shower
12	retired	7	shut (adj.)
2	rice	1	shut (past tense)
16	ridden	24-A	sickness
11	ride (v.)	12	sign (v.)
24-B	rights	16	silver
18	road	1	singer
18	roast	9	sixteenth
17	robe	9	sixth
16	rode	9	sixtieth
16	Romano (family name)	3	skiing
2	Rosa	3	skating
17	Rose	7	sky
5	rung (v.)	17	sleepwear
7	sad	20	sleeves
1	salad	7	slept
--	sale	17	slippers
12	for sale	24-A	smell
9	sales tax	18	sneeze
12	salesperson	16	so
18	sand	19	so...that
18	sandy	6	soap
5	sang	8	someone
16	sanitation worker	8	something
9	save	1	song
9	savings account	18	sore throat
4	saw (n.)	22	south
21	school	19	speed limit

1	spend	1	tomato
18	spend time	16	Tony
1	spent	17	took
17	spoke	4	<u>Tools and Equipment</u>
17	spoken	6	toothbrush
9	sponge	6	toothpaste
20	sportshirt	20	torn
18	spring	24-A	touch
10	state (n.)	6	towel
16	steal	23-B	train (v.)
7	steering wheel	9	trash can
9	Steve	7	trees
2	stick (of butter)	24-A	trust
5	still	15	turns
16	stole	9	twelfth
16	stolen	9	twentieth
24-A	Sullivan, Anne	3	twice
18	summer	23-B	unfriendly
5	sung	22	union (labor)
20	swear	10	United States
7	sweep	21	university
7	swept	21	until
20	swore	7	upset
20	sworn	9	vacuum (v.)
17	taken	9	vacuum cleaner
24-A	tame	2	vegetables
24-A	taste	24-B	violence
1	tea	24-B	violent
18	teapot	4	wait
10	teenager	22	wait for
4	teeth	22	wait on
9	tenth	17	wake
11	test	17	waked
11	tester	6	washcloth
10	Texas	24-B	Washington, D.C.
10	than	8	watermelon
9	that	18	way
5	themselves	5	wedding
13	"There, there"	22	west
9	third	4	when
9	thirteenth	12	while
9	thirtieth	13	why
19	threw	24-A	wild
18	throat	12	win
19	throw	7	wine
19	thrown	12	winner
13	ticket	18	winter
12	tie (in a race)	15	wives
--	time	17	woke
13	it takes time to	15	woman
13	it's time for	15	women
13	it's time to	23-A	wonder
14	timetable	4	wood
14	tired of	20	worn
18	toast	14	worried
18	toaster	15	worse

```
 8   worst
18   Would you mind...?
11   written
17   wrote
12   yard (measurement)
 5   yet
 5   yourself
 5   yourselves
19   zero
11   zip code number
```